THEATRE SYMPOSIUM
A PUBLICATION OF THE SOUTHEASTERN THEATRE CONFERENCE

Comedy Tonight!

Volume 16

Published by the

Southeastern Theatre Conference and

The University of Alabama Press

THEATRE SYMPOSIUM is published annually by the Southeastern Theatre Conference, Inc. (SETC), and by The University of Alabama Press. SETC nonstudent members receive the journal as a part of their membership under rules determined by SETC. For information on membership write to SETC, P.O. Box 9868, Greensboro, NC 27429-0868. All other inquiries regarding subscriptions, circulation, purchase of individual copies, and requests to reprint materials should be addressed to The University of Alabama Press, Box 870380, Tuscaloosa, AL 35487-0380.

THEATRE SYMPOSIUM publishes works of scholarship resulting from a single-topic meeting held on a southeastern university campus each spring. A call for papers to be presented at that meeting is widely publicized each autumn for the following spring. Information about the next symposium is available from the editor, Jay Malarcher, Division of Theatre and Dance, College of Creative Arts, West Virginia University, P.O. Box 6111, Morgantown, WV 26506-6111, jay. malarcher@mail.wvu.edu.

THEATRE SYMPOSIUM
A PUBLICATION OF THE SOUTHEASTERN THEATRE CONFERENCE

Volume 16 *Contents* **2008**

Introduction

COMEDY, AS A GENRE, defies categorization, strange as that may seem. A genre by its very nature defines a type and categorizes it, but through the centuries scholars, philosophers, and practitioners have attempted to classify and explain just what constitutes "comedy," "the comic," "humor," and the simple "funny." Always, though, some new variation emerges that challenges assumptions about comedy; for example, a romantic comedy may be a part of the genre, along with a parody of the same work: matter coexisting with antimatter, as it were.

The essays contained in this volume illustrate well the range of material that falls under the heading "comedy" as it is played on the stage. Certainly taste—or the lack thereof—plays a part in shaping the comedy of any period or place and contributes ultimately to its shelf life in the canon. Some works by Aristophanes still seem stageworthy, while others of his comedies may not register with an audience of today because of lost allusions . . . but rarely because of solved social problems: greed, jealousy, pomposity, and all the other human failings will always be found on the stage, as well as in boardrooms, living rooms, and the "seats" of government.

Tragedy, that most ponderous of genres, paradoxically acts on an audience's emotions, while comedy requires a rational interaction with the audience. Irony, paradox, incongruity, and juxtaposition—the building blocks of comedy—all require brain function in order to be appreciated, or even recognized.

Several of this volume's contributors have remarked in their essays that the surest way to kill a joke is to analyze it. It may be that because analysis must first take place in order simply to *get* the joke, any later analysis becomes superfluous. The brain, as any elementary physiology student can tell you, is the processor of information gathered from the senses, and it seems fitting, therefore, that this volume celebrates in many ways the sixth sense . . . the sense of humor, processed along with taste, smell, sight, hearing, and touch by the human mind. Mind? No, I don't mind at all.

The very first *Theatre Symposium* was devoted to commedia dell'arte performance, so this year's edition brings the subject full circle with a theme of comedy on stage, fittingly with a keynote essay by Stanley Vincent Longman, whose take on the commedia perfectly begins our exploration of the genre that Woody Allen has said eats at the children's table . . . even in the world of scholarship. Longman's "The Commedia dell'arte as the Quintessence of Comedy" introduces us to the inhabitants of "Commediatown," descendants of the Greeks and ancestors, it seems, of almost everyone who came after. The comic DNA, not to mention the tricks and machinations of these familiar types, lives on—literally—everywhere human beings have built up "civilized" society. Boris Senker, an eyewitness to the changes in Croatia from the Communist regime through the democratization of the last twenty years, reports in "Creating New Comic Stereotypes on the Croatian Postwar/Transition Stage" on the all-too-real stereotypes that have inherited many of the commedia masks' bad habits and have found their way onto the stage in his homeland. Trust that these types will not seem foreign at all.

One of the qualities of commedia that has intrigued spectators throughout history has to be the improvisational quality of the comedy. Audiences no doubt enjoy the risk performers take in working in such an impromptu manner, and most of the characters (truth be told) are so caught up in a web of lies, they're improvising themselves into deeper trouble at the same time. Patrick Bynane's "A Method to the Madness: Laughter Research, Comedy Training, and Improv" offers a contemporary take on the craft of improvisation. Hearkening back to some of the earliest comic traditions made new again, Diana Calderazzo's "Comedy Tonight . . . and Tomorrow: *A Funny Thing Happened on the Way to the Forum* and Laughter through the Ages" examines the roots of laughter and the expectations inherent in presenting "old shtick" to a new generation . . . or a new millennium.

Another classic laugh getter, Molière, is the subject of some nuts-and-bolts technique from Biliana Stoytcheva-Horissian in her "Performing Molière's Comedies: Challenges and Approaches." One cannot help but be amazed by the variety of ways that the great writers of comedy generate laughs and a greater understanding of human foibles, using physical and verbal elements to enhance the perspective on the world that comedy embraces. Staying with the French, Felicia J. Ruff's "The Laugh Factory? Humor and Horror at Le Théâtre du Grand Guignol" examines how the macabre can produce laughs, whether intentionally or not. How might the very neoclassical Molière have reacted to the Grand Guignol? With a rhymed couplet, no doubt.

Speaking of reaction to comedy, Henry Fielding, arguably the theatre practitioner most responsible for the British government's crackdown on subversive material, is the subject of Steven Dedalus Burch's essay, "When Satire More Than Closed on Saturday Night: Henry Fielding and the Licensing Act of 1737." *That* particular reaction lasted until 1968, but since then the British theatre has more openness at venues such as the Royal Court, where some of Samuel Beckett's most celebrated works met audiences for the first time. Christopher Morrison has dissected certain Beckett play texts for their connection to the comedy theory of Henri Bergson in "Meat, Bones, and Laughter without Words: Finding Bergson's *Laughter* in Beckett's *Act without Words I*."

Two contemporary writers form the basis for the next two essays, which also look critically at the mechanisms for generating laughter. First, E. Bert Wallace's "'The Ptydepe Word Meaning 'Wombat' Has 319 Letters': An Information-Age View of Technology and Satire in the Works of Václav Havel" investigates the ability for satire—even satire that replaces our known world—to seem uncomfortably familiar. Next, Luc Gilleman's essay, "Terry Johnson's *Hysteria:* Laughter on the Abyss of Insight," examines the presentation of Sigmund Freud in all of his iconic luster.

Finally, should anyone wish to take on comedy in a personal way, the experience and analysis of Broderick D. V. Chow in what he calls "DIY" comedy forms the basis of "Situations, Happenings, Gatherings, Laughter: Emergent British Stand-Up Comedy in Sociopolitical Context." The essays contained in this year's *Theatre Symposium* provide just a glimpse into the possibilities for comedy on the stage. If the past examples allow for extrapolation into the future, the position of comedy as a means of communicating problems and solutions for society's woes is remarkably sound. Amazing the veritable feast one might enjoy at the children's table!

The subject of comedy is, of course, an enjoyable one to consider in such a collegial atmosphere as the Theatre Symposium event, where the contributors shared their ideas in a congenial atmosphere at the historic Hotel Morgan in Morgantown, West Virginia, in April 2007. The essays that follow reflect the hard work that scholars smile through in studying comedy. I must, though, take the time to thank the many people and institutions that have assisted in the two parts of the *Theatre Symposium:* the live event and this journal.

First, the Southeastern Theatre Conference, which provides such a stable and inviting structure to this endeavor, especially Betsey Baun and her executive forces at work there, and also to Dan Waterman and his colleagues at the University of Alabama Press, for their attention to the detail work that makes each issue possible.

Heartfelt thanks, too, to the members of the *Theatre Symposium* Steering Committee and the Publications Committee for their advice and oversight, especially Phil Hill and Shelly Elman. To my predecessor as editor, Scott Phillips, and my associate editor, J. K. Curry, for support in the trenches as needed.

I have to thank my colleagues and the administration at West Virginia University, who so ably assisted in hosting the event in Morgantown and allowed the attendees to take in a performance of *The Philadelphia Story* during the conference's weekend of activities.

Finally, and most of all, my thanks to the contributors of the very fine essays contained herein, as well as everyone else who made the Morgantown event such a fun and edifying experience in the great tradition of the *Theatre Symposium.*

JAY MALARCHER
WEST VIRGINIA UNIVERSITY

The Commedia dell'arte as the Quintessence of Comedy

Stanley Vincent Longman

L AUGHTER IS peculiar to human beings. Other creatures do not indulge in it at all. A dog may be said to have a sense of humor as he tosses a ball in the air or invents games with his toys. We might say that tail wagging is canine laughter, but it is not the same as comic laughter. Comic laughter comes out of our awareness of the act of living, an awareness that is distinctly human. Living carries with it all sorts of difficulties and petty annoyances, but we carry on as best we can. Still, an abrupt recognition of something uncomfortable in another's experience can produce a laugh. We are not directly involved in the discomfort in someone else's experience (or in our own once we gain distance on it: "Someday we'll laugh about all this!"), so we are pleased to let someone else do the suffering. And comedy really is about suffering. This goes some way to explain the rebuke a certain vaudevillian (some attribute it to Bert Lahr) made to his audience when he had them all rolling in the aisles in gales of laugher: he came down to the lip of the stage, glared at the audience until they came to a stop and then scolded them in no uncertain terms: "You can laugh if you like, but this is funny!"

The Theatre Symposium this year (2007) has set itself the task of probing the nature of comedy and human laughter in all seriousness. Twenty-five hundred years ago there was another symposium at Agathon's house, where Socrates and friends explored the nature of human love. Plato recorded the nightlong discussion in his dialogue *The Symposium*. He reports that toward morning, all the guests had left except Agathon, the writer of tragedies, and Aristophanes, the writer of comedies. It was at that point that Socrates "compelled the other two to acknowledge that the genius of comedy was the same with that of tragedy, and that the true artist in tragedy was an artist in comedy also. To this they were constrained to assent, being drowsy, and not quite following the argument. And first of all Aristophanes dropped off."[1] Socrates managed to put the great comic Aristophanes to sleep simply by bringing up the subject of comedy. After all, comedy, once thoroughly analyzed, is a very serious matter.

So we will never know what Socrates thought of comedy. He was always a bit of a tease, anyway. In fact, he was something of a comic figure: he played the fool, asked annoying and simple-minded questions, feigned ignorance. Maurice Charney describes him as "uncouth, a notable drinker, convivial, hearty, bluff, candid and a man driven out of his home by a shrewish wife, Xanthippe."[2]

One way in which we may see the nature of comedy all these years later is by examining the commedia dell'arte. It is part of a long tradition, with roots dating back at least to the time of Aristophanes and with new branches extending into our own time. That tradition of the commedia, as it developed in Italy in the sixteenth century and went on refining itself through the eighteenth, came to embody concisely and vividly the quintessence of comedy. It would be profitable to see how newer comedy and critics and theorists relate to the commedia.

Fundamental to comedy and to the commedia is the portrayal of men and women as social beings, characters caught up in, and at odds with, society. In this sense the stage represents a miniature society, what L. J. Potts has called a "comic microcosm."[3] A couplet by William Blake sums up the difference between the tragic and the comic: "Great things are done when men and mountains meet; / This is not done by jostling in the streets."[4]

"Jostling in the streets" is an apt description of the commedia. The characters of the commedia live in their own little city. It is a self-contained city set apart from our world and operating under its own laws. The city has a population of undying characters whom you would meet the moment you entered the city gates. They are people caught up in a sort of time warp that prevents them from ever escaping their fixed identities or breaking out of patterns of behavior so ingrained as to repeat themselves in endless variations. Inside that world frustrations arise out of hunger (or deprivation), sex (or love), and power (the exercise of it or the thwarting of it). To paraphrase Jean-Paul Sartre, "Comedy is other people." Very early in the Cirque du Soleil show *La belle expérience,* a man, a sort of everyman, meets a tight group of other people. One of them tentatively approaches the man, who sticks out his hand as if for a handshake. This so frightens the other one that he returns to his group, none of whom can make out what that extended hand meant.

The encounter is unsettling, as the group chatters in gibberish about the apparent threat. The man is left nonplussed. It is both mystifying and funny. The chattering, in fact, is the commedia device of *grammelot,* nonsense syllables that nevertheless make a certain sense. Dario Fo, the great comic actor who has revived the spirit of the commedia in our own time, shows himself a master of the device in such plays as his *Mistero Buffo.* The multiple dialects of the commedia (Venetian, Bergamasque, Bolognese, and Neapolitan) would themselves have been gibberish for most audiences.

Commediatown, as we might call it, has a rigid social structure, based on power and money. At the top of the hierarchy are the *padroni,* the masters, the bosses. Chief among them are Pantalone, the rich Venetian merchant, and the Dottore, the Bolognese intellectual bully. Pantalone is a "magnifico," meaning that he occupies a position that requires him to look after the less fortunate. He is appropriately named Pantalone de' Bisognosi ("Pantalone of the needy ones"), but, of course, he is so miserly and self-centered that he is of no use to anyone. The Dottore is also self-absorbed, lording it over others by concocting outlandish lectures on the nature of things. A third sometimes joins these two as a padrone, namely the Capitano, the Neapolitan swaggering warrior, who boasts about his prowess on the battlefield as in the boudoir but who almost always proves to be a shrinking coward, impotent in both arenas. His full name is also indicative: Spavento dal Val d'Inferno or "The Shock Out of the Valley of Hell." Midway down in the power pyramid of Commediatown are the *innamorati,* the lovers, who have some privileges as sons or daughters of the padroni but who are mercilessly in their parents' control. They have all variety of pleasant and charming names such as Lelio and Clarice, Silvio and Isabella, Leandro and Flaminia. They are hopelessly in love, the more so for their inability to outmaneuver their parents. They are not very clever and have to turn to the servants, the *zanni,* to solve their dilemmas. At the very bottom, then, are the zanni, short for Giovanni and Gianni (making them "Johns"). They are always hungry, penniless, powerless, clawing for even some meager satisfaction. There are scores of these characters—Zanni, Arlecchino, Truffaldino, Fritellino, Faggiolino, Brighella, Pulcinella—all with varying degrees of wiliness, wit, ignorance, and stupidity. On the distaff side (also called zanni), with names like Colombina, Smeraldina, and Franceschina, are characters who are universally more clever and resourceful than virtually anyone in Commediatown.

All in all it is a vicious world, this city of the commedia. Its citizens scrap, fight, maneuver, and manipulate. They abuse each other in any way that they can. Yet there is one thing that invariably produces shared pleasure, if only momentarily: love. All said and done, the union of the lovers, the innamorati, is a joyous moment that causes everyone to forget his or her self-serving pettiness. Such moments do not last long—but at least they occur at the end.

We who sit outside their world have some comfort just by virtue of being outside. Nevertheless, there is such a thing as "comic empathy" despite claims that the comic audience laughs out of a sense of superiority. Comic empathy is a paradoxical sensation. At one and the same time, we may guffaw at and weep for the characters. Laurel and Hardy, in their 1932 film *The Music Box,* have the daunting task of delivering a huge player piano to a house at the top of an absurdly long and steep set of stairs. We groan and guffaw at each new scheme the two clowns hatch to get the piano up all those steps, but we also find ourselves vicariously engaged in their frustrations and earnest endeavors. We relish every one of their setbacks, and still we want them to win. Watching the piano tumble back down to the bottom of the hill after all that effort reminds us of poor Sisyphus.

At the most rudimentary level, characters in the commedia and in comedy generally have trouble with things. In fact, things can sometimes become characters and assume a life of their own, while characters may become things. Here is one example, Arlecchino and his slapstick:

ARLECCHINO: Oh misery and woe is me! The Dottore is marrying my dear Colombina and that means I'll have to live without her. No, I tell you, I'd rather die! Oh you old goat, you stupid Dottore! And you, Colombina: your affections run like straws in the wind. And I am left to suffer. I shall go for a quick and spectacular death. It will be recorded in all the histories of our time. I'll get a rope, make a noose, put it around my neck, put the rope over a rafter, get a chair then kick the chair out from under me and . . . aarrrgh!
(He mimes choking to death. His slapstick starts to talk to him.)
SLAPSTICK: What's the matter with you, you dunce! Why should you kill yourself over a silly woman?
ARLECCHINO *(earnestly)*: Well, she has done a terrible thing.
SLAPSTICK: So, once you're hung, will you be any better off?
ARLECCHINO: No, I'll be worse off. But once I hang myself, she'll be sorry.
SLAPSTICK: Once you're dead, you won't know about that one way or the other.
ARLECCHINO: I am going to do it.
SLAPSTICK: Oh, no, you're not.
ARLECCHINO: On yes I am! Here I go!
SLAPSTICK: And here I am to beat some sense into you. Take that . . . and that . . . and that!
(The Stick beats Arlecchino all over the place.)[5]

The same phenomenon appears in comedies from time immemorial: custard pies, wooden planks, unicycles, telephones, tangled ropes, and so forth. Charlie Chaplin had extraordinary comic encounters with things in his films. Often he exhibits a strange kind of aplomb in these encounters, as if accepting stoically the situation dictated by the objects. In his 1916 film *The Pawnshop*, the object is a long ladder. He is simply going about his business of cleaning the front of the store, but the ladder becomes virtually a character in the action. The ladder catches his colleague between two rungs as Charlie marches out of the storeroom to the front of the store. From that moment on the ladder dictates the comic business between Charlie and the man and the policeman who interrupts. Something similar happens with Monsieur Hulot's kayak in Jacques Tati's film, *Monsieur Hulot's Holiday* (1954). Hulot takes his damaged kayak out to sea, paddling about near the shore. Suddenly, the little boat snaps in the middle and the stern flips over on the prow, trapping him inside. His attempts to free himself create a spectacle resembling the snapping jaws of a sea monster. The sight frightens everyone on the beach so much that they flee for cover.

Both Henri Bergson and Suzanne Langer find comedy in the assertion of a living spirit, or *élan vital*, against an alien or uncaring world. Bergson calls laughter a "social corrective," arguing first that society (despite its strictures) values the human capacity to adjust, to assume a natural vitality. The moment we see that capacity thwarted by the imposition of the mechanical, we are likely to laugh. His famous phrase descriptive of the comic spectacle is "something mechanical encrusted on the living," and we laugh, "every time a person gives us the impression of being a thing."[6] In other words, the comic derives from a sudden awareness of rigidity where we ought to find vitality. Of course, the most blatant examples of this are such moments as the dignified man stepping on a banana peel, tumbling over and landing on his butt. "Slapstick" comedy is always based on abrupt reminders of our physicality. And, of course, we associate that instrument, the slapstick, with the commedia dell'arte.

Langer makes similar observations. Living creatures, she says, "live by opportunities, in a world fraught with disasters." She sees comedy as arising out of the natural human "life-feeling" set against a "world that is, above all, intricate and puzzling," and she concludes: "The feeling of comedy is a feeling of heightened vitality, challenged wit and will, engaged in the great game with Chance."[7]

To return to Commediatown: the masks and costumes of the characters vividly illustrate Bergson's and Langer's principle. Each character is defined by his mask and costume. This produces tension at once between the fixed mask and the actor under it. These are half masks that leave open the lower part of the actor's face, his mouth and chin, and that provide narrow holes for the eyes, forcing the actor to turn his head directly to whatever he wants to see. Moreover, the costume, along with the mask, dictates a pose and movement that cannot be escaped. Put on one of these masks, and the body responds at once. The whole demeanor and attitude emerge as a natural response to the cues taken from the mask. It is a clear case of Bergson's notion of something "mechanical encrusted on the living . . . a rigidity applied to the mobility of life."[8] In fact, he speaks of garments, saying that fashions out of the past often appear ludicrous in the present. Any of us living today who also lived through the 1970s cringe at the photos taken then with the bushy hair, sideburns, and green leisure suits or stringy hair, braless bosoms, and slinky skirts.

In keeping with Langer's notion of an intricate and puzzling world and the great game of Chance, hunger (or deprivation) is the first and most basic drive that fuels the action in commedia. In fact it may have been the first to appear. One theory has it that sometime in the early 1500s, during a time of war and famine, peasants from the hills came down into the Po valley in search of work, food, and money. This is the story of Il Ruzzante, the stock character invented by Angelo Beolco. He appears in Beolco's plays as a long-suffering peasant, a conscripted soldier, and an unhappy cuckold suffering abuse from both the war and his wife. Dario Fo has created his own version of the starved Ruzzante in his famous *Mistero Buffo*. He explodes with cries of hunger, speaking a wild and excited *grammelot* as he imagines himself eating himself, his eyeball, his foot, his hand, his entrails, even his mouth, then reaching out to gobble up the audience, the mountains, and finally God Himself, who allowed such suffering to take place. He then conjures an enormous feast in two great boiling (and imaginary) cauldrons only to have it all evaporate in front of him. And to finish, he plays the famous commedia "Lazzi of the Fly," in which he chases a buzzing fly around, seeing it light on various audience members' heads, then catching it and eating it with great relish.

Hunger shows up in many of the *lazzi* or stock pieces of business of the commedia. It also appears in several of Charlie Chaplin's films. In *The Tramp* (1915) we see him watching a man on the other side of a restaurant window eat a steak, and, in complete harmony, he conjures his own steak in pantomime and eats it out on the street. In *The Gold Rush* (1925) he serves up a feast in the form of a boiled shoe and does so with elegant aplomb out of all proportion to the culinary object.

Sex, of course, is more complicated than food because now we are dealing with the individual in society. In that party reported in *The Symposium*, Aristophanes tells his version of the origin of love. He explains that there were once primordial creatures with two heads, four arms, and four legs whom Zeus cut in two and the two halves have ever since been trying to reunite.[9] The same author had good fun with the embarrassment of male urgency in the play *Lysistrata*. Men and women baffle each other continually while also needing each other desperately. L. J. Potts asserts:

> It is not surprising that easily the favourite topic of comedy is sex. In no other department of life is there more "jostling." And nowhere else can we *all* be said to be eccentric; but here we can. All women appear abnormal to all men, and all men to all women; and rightly, for sex carries with it specialization and so a departure from the *common* human pattern. This departure is accentuated in civilised life. There is a wide gap between the impulses that precede and accompany human mating, and codes of manners and sentiment between men and women that prevail from time to time.[10]

Much of what makes sex comical comes of its sheer awkwardness. It is a nuisance, as Potts also points out, and "we all sometimes wish we could dispense with it. But there it is; and just as the poets have paid tribute to its noblest and most beautiful manifestations and also reviled it for cruelties and humiliations, so let the comic writers enjoy it as the greatest of eternal jokes" (ibid., 57).

The commedia depicts all sorts of warfare in the "battle of the sexes." The two innamorati constantly find themselves at odds through misunderstandings, jealousies, and deceptions. They have not only the problem of their parents' plans running contrary to their union; they have each other. So they are constantly rejecting one another and reconciling. Here is an example, designating the characters simply as "he" and "she":

HE. So you are willing to do whatever your old man tells you to do?
SHE. A good daughter is always obedient.
HE. Even if you're told to marry the old Dottore?
SHE. What am I supposed to do?
HE. Did he tell you to marry that old windbag?
SHE. Yes. That's why I came to you. I'm at a loss how to get out of it.
HE. So you'll just go ahead and pack your things and move in with that fat old fart?
SHE. I didn't say that.
HE. You said you are always obedient.
SHE. True. Help me.
HE. If you're so willing, it must mean you no longer care for me.
SHE. Of course I care for you.

HE. Not if you can decide so easily to go along with this outrageous plan.

SHE. It's not so easy.

HE. You don't love me anymore.

SHE. You wouldn't say that if you still loved me.

HE. I've had it with you. I know someone who would be happy to have me since you don't care.

SHE. Go ahead. Run to her. I'm through with you.

HE. This is good-bye, then. *(He starts to leave.)*

SHE. Good riddance.

HE. *(He comes back.)* Did you say something?

SHE. You wish!

HE. I'm going then. I am stepping out of your life. *(He is going, ever so slowly.)*

SHE. Step as far as you like. In fact I'll step out of yours. (She starts to exit the opposite direction, looking back as she goes. They are both gone. After a few moments, they reappear.)

HE. Aha! You're back, then.

SHE. So that's as far as you're going to step . . .

They can go on like this for a good long time. This exchange is typical of the lovers' spats found all through the commedia. This particular one is very like an exchange between Valère and Mariane in *Tartuffe,* but in that case Molière gets Dorine to function as a comic go-between. Of course, the lovers will always reconcile, just as Mariane and Valère do, and the play will end with their happy marriage.

Sex in a more literal sense appears as the various zanni chase after their female counterparts. There are times when Arlecchino cannot make up his mind whether to eat the food on a plate to his right-hand side or go after Franceschina bending over her laundry on his left. There is a scene in the pilot episode of *M*A*S*H* in which Hawkeye and Trapper John (like Brighella and Arlecchino) connive to arrange for a lottery to raise money, using as the winner's reward a date with a sexy nurse. As if to demonstrate how apt their choice of the sexy nurse is, a montage of Hawkeye pursuing her appears in the midst of their wheeling and dealing.

And then there is Pantalone's overt lechery. Here his old age is an uncomfortable impediment. He assumes and hopes that his wealth more than makes up for his diminished manhood. Symbolic of that is the heavy moneybag that dangles between his legs. Just as Arlecchino has trouble making up his mind, Pantalone worries about the value of money as against a sexual encounter. Here he is worrying:

Hee hee, let me tell you something confidentially. *(He says this to the audience in a stage whisper and looks around to be sure no one is listening.)* I just fooled that dumb sap Ruffiano into thinking he'd have to give me two gold crowns if he expected a good rate of interest on any loan from me. See? Here they are: two gold crowns. I am going to put them with the other coins I have in this beautiful bag. *(He drops the two in and feels the heft of his bag.)* I'll empty the coins in the secret basement of my house along with all my other coins. I can then watch the pile grow bigger and taller all the time. I like the idea of things growing bigger and taller. *(He seems to relish the tumescent pile of money before his eyes. Then his eyes wander and he sees a pretty woman.)* Ooh, you're a tasty little piece of pastry, a lovely jiggly pudding I'd like to put my spoon in. You wouldn't fancy dallying with a man of my prowess, now would you? No? *(He starts to give up, then returns to her.)* You aren't for sale, by any chance? I have a couple of gold crowns. I could let you have . . . one of them. Oh no, wait a minute! That's too much! How about three or four sequins? Nothing doing, you say? No, I can't afford them either. Oh well, good things come and go. At least I still have my two gold crowns.

There are many such temptations for Pantalone, who in some instances insists on marrying the young girl himself rather than see his son have her.

Finally, we come to the third of the three driving forces, power. Unlike hunger, which is more or less private *(even if brought on by society)*, or sex, which is at any rate personal, power cuts across the whole society. It brings the whole of Commediatown into the fray. The dominance of the padroni is capricious and self-serving, causing no small amount of suffering for the zanni and the innamorati alike. Pantalone, especially, but also the Dottore and sometimes the Capitano abuse power, hold on to their positions as a matter of long-standing tradition, and now they are useless, weak, worn out, distracted. Yet they remain entrenched. The commedia is about rebellion and usurpation as much as anything. This is a pattern one finds in all comedy from ancient farce through high drawing room comedy. You see it in *The Farce of Master Pierre Pathelin*, as well as in *The Importance of Being Earnest.*

Northrop Frye has some interesting observations on this score. For him, comedy deals with the overthrow of one social order and the establishment of another. The old social order gives the power to characters whose age or thought renders them weak and unfit. They are in bondage to old habits and rituals and worn-out laws: they are usurpers or *alazons,* who must themselves be usurped by the young, the subservient, the *eirons,* and the self-deprecators. It is generally true of the commedia that it is the zanni who bring about a change in the social order, and they do it by outwitting and by one-upmanship. This competition accounts for the tricks, disguisings, impersonations, and elaborate lies zanni typically employ against the masters. Speaking of comedy, generally, Maurice Charney says:

Irony may be a survival technique, but it is comic because of a gross dispro-
portion between subject and object. . . . It looks as if the ironic fool will,
through a cunning display of meekness, inherit the earth. Winner take all,
but how can you cope with a winner who looks like a loser? The confusion
is deliberate. The ironic fool is a master of disguise who cultivates illusions
and false appearances. Wariness is all: be on your guard, don't let your de-
fenses down—and there seems to be an automatic assumption that life is a
struggle between ill-matched forces, in which the weakest always wins.[11]

Of course, to aid in the game, the weaknesses of the masters, the
padroni, are there to be seized on: Pantalone's miserliness and lechery,
the Dottore's puffed-up pedantry, and the Capitano's cowardice. For
our part as audience, the turning of the tables is a prospect we antici-
pate and relish. Comedy gets its name from the ritual of *comus,* which
in essence is celebration uniting everyone. And it can only happen once
the hypocrite and the poseur are exposed. Then we can all celebrate our
mutual humanity.

Frye describes the pattern of social upheaval as basic to comedy. The
society we encounter at the outset of the play must change; we know it
must. He describes the comic action in this way:

The movement of comedy is usually a movement from one kind of society to another. At the beginning of the play, the obstructing characters
are in charge of the play's society, and the audience recognizes that they
are usurpers. At the end of the play the device in the plot that brings hero
and heroine together causes a new society to crystallize around the hero,
and the moment when this crystallization occurs is the point of resolution
in the action.[12]

This brings us to an important paradox. The world of the commedia is
its own self-contained world encased in its rigid forms and stuck behind
the city walls. Yet at the same time it is an open, free form that not only
acknowledges the audience but incorporates that outer world into its
world. The characters make frequent appeals to the audience. A typical
device is the so-called *slittamento,* the sudden breaking of stage action
to address the audience. Anyone in the audience could suddenly become
the butt of the comic action. Someone sneezes and Dario Fo incorporates it in the show. Someone else snores and Ettore Petrolini enjoins
the fellow's neighbor to nudge him. Or someone coughs and Antonio
Fava stops all the action. Still another one giggles and Alessandro Mar-
chetti stares at him and says, "You laughing at me?" These characters
have a remarkable capacity for reaching out to the audience while maintaining their own world. A zanni may make disparaging remarks about

his master but shares them as an aside with the audience. In the battle for control, every character wants to enlist us on his or her side. Each actor assumes a double focus, one looking at the fellows onstage, the other outward to the audience, especially when the going gets tough. This is not a matter of mugging or playing to the audience; it has to do with the uncomfortable, awkward, and therefore comic moments that are hard to deal with. It is as though the character (not the actor) wants some reassurance or clarification from us. Eventually, after all, it is we who exert the final force to produce the new social order at the end. To quote Frye once again: "The resolution of comedy comes, so to speak, from the audience's side of the stage; in a tragedy it comes from some mysterious world on the opposite side."[13]

Beyond the audience's side of the stage is the bigger world, their society. It is the macrocosm that is host to the comic microcosm. In other words, Commediatown is a world contained within the larger world of the assembled audience. As such, it can reflect, mimic, and mock that world. The fixed and rigid nature of Commediatown stands in contrast to the improvisation the actors employ. It was a regular practice for commedia troupes to send an advance man forward to sound out the issues and controversies in the next city in which they would play. Franca Rame, Dario Fo's colleague in marriage as well as onstage, is a *figlia d'arte* who remembers how her parents' company incorporated the local personalities in each town they visited. The commedia is improvisational in that every show will alter itself as it goes, tapping into and enlarging the world it encounters. With that freedom the scenario can pull anything from the outside world into its own little world. The audience can be expected to recognize and delight in such references. So one might say that this Italian commedia is structured like Chinese boxes: the inner world of the play within the outer world of the audience within the world beyond. Comedies generally, not just the commedia, play on our awareness of the larger world, the society in which we live. Without that resonance a comedy goes flat.

Perhaps the best-known versions of Chinese boxes in comedy are found in the plays of Molière, who developed his dramaturgy out of the commedia dell'arte. *Tartuffe,* for example, is set in the house of Orgon, which Tartuffe has taken over as the audience watches in the theatre house, fully aware that this interloper must be driven out. We are very aware of his hypocrisy and lechery. He is a mixture of Pantalone and Dottore, and he might very well have counterparts seated in boxes out in the theatre house. Moreover, the takeover of the house of Orgon had a strong parallel in the takeover of the House of France by the Company of the Holy Sacrament. Played in any society, the larger house is certain to have "Tartuffes" at work undermining the rest of us. This is the excuse for the king's intervention in the play, arresting Tartuffe and liberating the house of Orgon.

When you think of the elaborate specious arguments Tartuffe concocts in his effort to seduce Orgon's wife, Elmire, one is reminded of the lengthy and elaborate speeches the Dottore would concoct. In the following example the Dottore launches into a learned discourse only to regain dignity after tripping over a little rock in the street. Nevertheless, it illustrates how the character seeks to control us and how unwilling we are to accept him:

> Now you see me standing here. I shall now peregrinate, perambulate, migrate, and mosey to that spot over there. (He does so in grand dignity, but as he goes, he trips on a small stone. He looks up to see if anyone noticed and in embarrassment he launches into this account.) There you see that I have slipped on this pebble and pebbles, as you may know, are made of stone. Stone is a major ingredient in the composition of the earth. The earth is round as is this pebble and, inasmuch as they both are made of stone, they share also that common characteristic. Stone also is the essential substance of Greece and Greece is the home of Alexander the Great, and Alexander the Great was the great master of all the earth. His teacher was Aristotle who has taught us that a strong mind requires a strong body. And a strong body is what Atlas has. Indeed he is so strong that he holds up the whole earth with the great pillars of Gibraltar, which is a rock whose essential substance is stone, and stone, as I have pointed out, is the essential substance of this pebble.

Roberto Benigni has created a contemporary version of a Dottore sham lecture in the movie *Life Is Beautiful*. Benigni's character has taken a fancy to a schoolteacher and goes to her school pretending to be the expected dignitary from the Fascist Ministry of Education. He arrives at the school before the appointed hour and manages a quick confidential chat with the woman and then finds himself forced into giving the little pupils a lecture on the superiority of the Italian race. He first demonstrates the elegance of his ear lobe and ends up half undressed singing the praises of his belly button. It is at that moment that the real emissary from the Ministry of Education appears, and Benigni makes his "Aryan" retreat.

A film, of course, is a contained medium that plays to an audience out in the dark of the auditorium. But in this sequence the pupils represent the immediate world of the audience and the fascist regime, along with its "racist scientists," the world beyond.

Over the course of the last century the three-realm structure of comedy underwent some strong alterations. Stage realism of the first half of the twentieth century tended to squelch the use of the second realm, the immediate world of the audience. The fourth wall insisted on the audience's staying well beyond the stage action. Then, in the second half of the century, the tone of plays shifted dramatically. Much of this was foreshadowed by Luigi Pirandello, Bertolt Brecht, and others, but a new tone emerged strongly after midcentury. Now the world beyond became far more important, and it assumed dimensions and qualities it had never had before. The characters onstage may still be comical, but their encounter with the difficulties and awkwardness of living was something much more powerful. Albert Camus' reference to the myth of Sisyphus is appropriate, and it is no accident that Martin Esslin made it the basis of his analysis of the Theatre of the Absurd. The man condemned to push a boulder to the top of a hill only to see it roll back to the bottom is a comic image if it weren't for the feeling of metaphysical alienation that accompanies it. Vladimir and Estragon waiting for Godot give us some priceless moments of comic action, yet when all is said and done, the mysteries of their world go well beyond the boundaries of an unjust or corrupt society. It becomes an inexplicable world with impersonal power over its occupants. Something the same could be said of Rosencrantz and Guildenstern. In one sense we seem not far from Laurel and Hardy and their piano; in another we are miles away from them. As Robert Corrigan has pointed out, we have been experiencing a blurring of the boundary between tragedy and comedy: Corrigan ends his essay noting the blurring of the boundary between tragedy and comedy: "One of the most striking characteristics of the modern drama is the way in which the age-old distinctions between the tragic and the comic (the serious and the ludicrous, the painful and the painless) have been obliterated." The comic begins to serve a different function than it has for so long fulfilled. Corrigan again: "Whereas in the comedy of earlier times, comic means were used to comic ends, in the modern theatre comic means are employed to serious ends. The comic has become a transparency through which we see to the serious."[14]

Notes

1. Plato, *The Symposium,* in *The Dialogues of Plato,* trans. Benjamin Jowett (Chicago: Encyclopedia Britannica, 1952), 173.

2. Maurice Charney, *Comedy High and Low* (New York: Oxford University Press, 1978), 11.

3. L. J. Potts, *Comedy* (London: Hutchinson's University Library, 1950), 61.

4. Quoted in ibid., 49.

5. Variations of this and other monologues and dialogues appear in John Rudlin, *Commedia dell'Arte: An Actor's Handbook* (London: Routledge, 1994). All would originally have been improvised. See also Anthony Caputi, *Buffo: The Genius of Vulgar Comedy* (Detroit: Wayne State University Press, 1978).

6. Henri Bergson, *Laughter: An Essay on the Meaning of the Comic,* trans. Cloudesley Bereton and Fred Rothwell (New York: Macmillan, 1937), 58.

7. Suzanne Langer, *Feeling and Form: A Theory of Art* (New York: Charles Scribner's Sons, 1953), 329, 330, 348–49.

8. Bergson, *Laughter,* 37–38.

9. Plato, *The Symposium,* 157–59.

10. Potts, *Comedy,* 49–50.

11. Charney, *Comedy High and Low,* 12.

12. Northrop Frye, *Anatomy of Criticism* (Princeton, NJ: Princeton University Press, 1957), 163.

13. Ibid., 164.

14. Robert W. Corrigan, "Comedy and the Comic Spirit," in *Comedy: Meaning and Form,* ed. Robert Corrigan (Scranton, PA: Chandler Publishing, 1965), 9, 11.

Creating New Comic Stereotypes on the Croatian Postwar/Transition Stage

Boris Senker

I N THE FIRST TWO decades of the socialist regime in post–World War II Yugoslavia, the number of public theatres in what is now Croatia substantially increased, and the state and local authorities preferred to see comedy used on the stage either for pure entertainment (that is, not raising ideological and political issues at all) or for constructive criticism of the new society in progress.[1] To fulfill these goals, two specialized theatres were founded in Zagreb: The Comedy Theatre (for "pure entertainment") and The Satirical Theatre (for "constructive criticism"). Croatian comic theatre artists did not accept these divisions, however. Instead, entertainment and criticism were mixed as the genre of "political farce" or "grotesque tragedy" became the core segment of a political theatre, which was subversive at least in its intentions and self-perception.[2] Understanding the stage as the best place for undertaking symbolic political and social actions, Croatian theatre from the mid-1950s until the late 1980s was preoccupied mostly with contemporary society and the unrecognized (officially) tensions between a discourse of force and a discourse of reason, politics and art, private truths and public lies, utopian projects and crude reality. In dealing with these issues, the comic theatre created a set of stock characters fashioned on contemporary social types such as, for example, Party Chief, (Young) Idealist, Turncoat, Fearful Dissident, Toady, Crook, Informer, Ideal Secretary, Honey Girl, Shrew, and so forth.[3]

Created onstage by the members of three, or perhaps four, generations of actresses and actors, each of these stereotypes underwent a series of formal changes, but some fundamental features—vocabulary, mimicry, gesture, significant costume items and/or props (as various attributes), even vocal characteristics—remained constant, making a preliminary identification of dramatis personae easier.

Party Chief of the early socialist period, for example, wore a long leather coat, leather visor cap, shirt without tie, and boots. He had a Stalinesque mustache, spoke in a deep, harsh voice, swore, pounded the table to show "who's the boss," treated all women as members of his unofficial harem, and drank and ate a lot. After the 1960s the leather coat and boots were replaced by a gray suit and red tie; the gestures became more polite, but the mentality and the language of this stereotype did not substantially change; and the heavy mustache remained the attribute of power and manliness.

An Idealist (mostly young and therefore uncorrupted) was Party Chief's regular antagonist. The Idealist was almost always a man because women were marginalized in Croatian political theatre, as well as in politics, and his appearance suggested a sort of blindness to reality, to everyday life, and a lack of practical skills: he wore spectacles, because he was short-sighted in all senses of the word, his clothes were shabby and out of any fashion, his worn-out briefcase a mix of papers, books, and magazines. His speeches were passionate and impressive but were given at the wrong place, in the wrong time, and for the wrong audience.

Having no personality and functioning as a distorted mirror and/or loudspeaker of the most powerful person, group, or organization in the represented community, Turncoat was one of the most despised characters, the object of mockery in both the comic theatre (by other characters) and in the society at large. His transformations were a chronicle of the political and ideological changes throughout his lifetime. All the past and present ideological discourses and patterns of behavior—especially monarchist, Stalinist, and Titoist—were stored in him, and each could be restored when expedient.[4]

The stereotype of the Fearful Dissident was characterized by a contrast between brave, radical criticism of official policy and fearful conduct: whispering, turning around, changing the subject of conversation or hurriedly leaving the stage at the first sign of any danger. Toady became a caricature of Party Chief: his voice was either goatish, or he stuttered; his mustache, for example, was more like a toothbrush or a comb than like the heavy Stalinesque mustache of his paragon; instead of pounding the table, he ominously raised his finger; instead of boots, he wore clumsy shoes; instead of a visor cap, he covered his head with a French beret, traditionally used in Croatian rural regions as neutral substitution for hats and caps that were conventional signs of profession, confession, and so forth. Later, he would wear a suit and tie almost identical to the boss's. In gestures he was the incarnation of the popular notion of a spineless person: his eyes and ears were always ready to catch his master's commanding gestures and words; he was the first to open the door for him, light his cigarette, or fetch him something. In short, he was disgustingly submissive and polite.

The Crook stereotype in Croatian comedies and satires was a distant descendant of two ancestors: Molière's Tartuffe and Gogol's Khlestakov. In the numerous Croatian revivals of Molière's *Tartuffe* and Gogol's *Inspector General,* the protagonists were always treated not as historical but as contemporary—or, to be more precise, still-existing—social types, both by directors and by leading actors. Stage interpretations of Tartuffe, Khlestakov, and their twentieth-century Croatian descendants changed through the forty years under discussion, but they always involved more or less obvious parody (lexical, paralinguistic, mimic, and gestic) of demagogic discourse and behavior, as well as of people's secret desires and illusions.

Finally, Informers were easy to recognize at first glance in the theatre. Dressed in long gray raincoats, they hid their faces behind spread newspapers, forgetting to turn pages.

Because politics was "man's business," there were few female stereotypes in that period and all were fashioned from the male point of view— playwright's, director's, or spectator's. An Ideal Secretary was the man's "right arm." Although her outlook changed on the stage, something remained constant: she was always characterized as a sexually unattractive, spinsterlike woman, dressed in a dull, unfashionable suit, with a conservative haircut, and almost always with spectacles and a notebook, ready to listen and write down her chief's words.

Quite the opposite, Honey Girl, a stage reincarnation of the past Middle-European *Süsse Mädel* stereotype, was the embodiment of men's fantasies and one who obviously worked on her body, behavior, and outlook to meet those fantasies. She was blond; wore a short, tight skirt, high heels, and heavy makeup; spoke in a sweet, childish way; and moved with a certain insecurity, as if she needed someone's strong arm to support her. The film industry—at the beginning Italian and French and, later, American—supplied Croatian actresses with the most important information on the best way to portray this stereotype. Because of the modeling, it sometimes became difficult to be positive about a performance: was an actress in a Honey Girl role trying to resemble this or that movie star in a similar role, or was she trying to show a fictional girl trying to act or to be like them?

Just as the comic theatre often treats marriage as life imprisonment for a free man, the Shrew embodied the worst punishment for characters like the Party Chief or Toady. She spoke loudly, had a deep voice, smoked, drank brandy, cared neither about the weight nor the shape of her body, and went around in curlers and a nightgown all day long. If she entered politics or public life either in contemporary comedies or updated older plays, she would dress like the Ideal Secretary, with a touch of a military uniform, and act like a Shrew at home.

As a rule, historical sets of comic stereotypes do not resemble accidental bunches of funny or ridiculous unrelated individuals. On the contrary, each of these sets, similar to the dramatis personae of individual plays, as Manfred Pfister's analysis of drama shows, tends to be organized as a kind of microsociety "structurally arranged and classified according to the qualitative correspondences and contrasts" among its members.[5] The underlying net of relations in such a microsociety is, as a rule, representation, interpretation, or deconstruction of the relations basic for the macrosociety *in which* and *for which* these stereotypes are impersonated onstage. The society to which the outlined set of comic stereotypes in Croatian theatre referred was based on political oppression, bureaucracy, repression of conflicts, distrust, fear, uniformity, and the silent solidarity of the oppressed.

The transition from the socialist political and economical system into the postsocialist one that took place at the very beginning of the 1990s was greatly desired but had unpredictable and violent results: the disintegration of Yugoslavia; the rise of nationalistic fervor; war in Croatia, Bosnia, and Kosovo; chaotic and unjust privatization; loss of traditional markets; unemployment; great migrations; the emergence of a new class; and new, undesired centers of power. Although the economical, political, social, and cultural environment substantially changed in the course of the fifteen years that followed, the administrative and financial position of public theatre institutions in Croatia remained more or less the same as it used to be before the war and transition. None of the public theatres was closed, and all of them continued to receive regular state and/or regional subsidies. In the first postwar and transition years, the majority of theatre people, fully protected as state, region, or city employees, thought that changes and conflicts were taking place somewhere outside, concerning others, and that they could carry on with the old acting routines, including comic ones.[6] That is why at first the majority of former comic stereotypes remained in use, only slightly and superficially redesigned. The most common misconception was that the best or the most popular among old political and social comedies—comedies of manners, let's say, dealing with private and public life under the socialist regime—could be easily updated and staged merely by replacing the old keywords of political and ideological discourse (working class, common interests, brotherhood and unity, proletarian internationalism, egalitarianism) with new ones (nation, democracy, political pluralism, global market, private property, free media) or by replacing old iconography (the red star, Tito's portrait) with a new one (the cross, national tricolor, and coat of arms), and that so adapted and actualized they would perfectly correspond with the changed and still changing society.

This did not work, however, and several productions of slightly adapted Croatian comedies from the 1970s and 1980s failed. At the same time, some foreign comedies, including De Filippo's *The Millions of Naples*, Ostrovsky's *It's a Family Affair— We'll Settle it Ourselves*, and Shakespeare's *The Taming of the Shrew*, for example, along with a few nineteenth-century Croatian satires on fixed elections, false patriotism, and scheming in high society, proved to be far more suitable for such actualizations, sometimes accomplished through performance without changing a single line.

After such experiences, Croatian actresses, actors, and directors realized that they had to forget about the past successes and start to work on the creation of a new set of comic stereotypes. The process is far from finished, partly because of the still-turbulent social, economic, and cultural scene and partly because of difficulties with the identification of paradigmatic social types and their characteristic features, namely their vocabulary, favorite music or topics of conversation, characteristic mimics, gestures and costumes, significant props, and so on.

Of course, some social/comic types have remained more or less unchanged. Turncoat, as the most adaptable person, and first to adapt to every change, is one of them. Shrew—as the eternal, unavoidable, and seldom-deserved man's punishment from the dominant patriarchal point of view—is another. But there is one important and significant cultural difference concerning the latter: the old Shrew had nothing to do with feminism. On the Croatian stage she was regularly presented as a person with completely neglected or undeveloped womanhood or, to be more precise, as a person with no sex appeal at all. The new Shrew is often presented as a person who has intentionally rejected her "natural" womanhood and acts like a man (and against men) by her own free choice.

Some stereotypes are rather easy to identify in society and fashion on the stage. False Patriot, for example, loudly and proudly pronounces words like *Croatia, Croatian, nation, history, tradition, freedom,* and so forth; he jumps to his feet as soon as he hears a tune resembling the national anthem and puts his right hand on his heart, while slipping, if possible, his left hand into his neighbor's pocket. As a young extremist, he can easily turn into a fascistlike Nationalist-Racist-Homophobe with shaven head, dressed in black trousers and black T-shirt, with visible tattoos on his arms and a big gold or silver cross on a necklace. Braggart

Soldier, the stereotype with a long history in this border area, is characterized by an army uniform, which he continues to wear despite the war's being over. He keeps telling stories about the horrors of war and boasting of his unbelievable deeds. His performance is rich with gestures, wild actions, and fearsome pauses in performance. He uses props and set to reconstruct the battlefield (that he probably never saw) on the stage.

A specific exchange between political and theatrical spheres took place in the creation of the New Statesman stereotype. Namely, at the very beginning of the 1990s, when Croatia was still not fully recognized as an independent state, the new government asked theatre people to collaborate with politicians and historians on the "invention of traditions" for the Croatian state.[7] For example, the uniforms of the President's Guard were designed by a theatre designer, and the changing of the guard was choreographed by a theatre choreographer. As new Croatian statesmen were fond of putting on newly designed sashes, a sash has become an almost inevitable attribute of the New Statesman stereotype in performances of comedies, Croatian and foreign, new and old alike. Lack of mimics, majestic postures and rigidity in words and actions have gradually become distinctive characteristics of this stereotype. The theatre had participated in its creation in reality and then started to laugh at the creation that was partly its own.

On the other hand, the stereotypes of Media Star, Barbie, and the like should be treated in the context of the growing and confusing impact of commercial television, film, video, and lifestyle magazines on everyday life in Croatia. At the same time, public theatre institutions and dramatic literature struggle desperately to keep their privileged position in the culture, still understood as strictly divided into "high" and "low" varieties. Through Media Star, Barbie, and some other stereotypes, the theatre mocks the people who mistake images from popular culture as reality and fashion themselves after them. Thus, it mocks confused people who dress, speak, and behave like their new idols from that recently discovered glamour world.

Some stereotypes are still vague, however, in this society, as well as in its theatre. One of them is the Nouveau Riche or Tycoon regularly seen with his personal Bodyguard and his Barbie-like wife by his side. In the early 1990s Tycoon was at first sight recognized on the stage by his short haircut, mobile phone (which he used to get information on his cargo of smuggled goods), and white socks that were, by prejudice of course, connected with the South Croatian rural region from which all Croatian tycoons were believed to come, not directly, but after years or even decades of emigration, mostly to Germany. As both audience and actors have become fed up with so simplistic and inadequate an interpretation of fundamental social changes, the search for better solutions has begun. Some of the most recent stage case studies of this stereotype were more than obviously inspired by Mexican, Colombian, Brazilian, and other widely popular *telenovelas*, which offer quite an impressive number of repulsive Nouveaux Riches in overly expensive suits and silk shirts, with too-colorful ties and too-shiny shoes, with oiled hair and thin mustaches. Though so easy to recognize, these types are hard to find anywhere off the stage or screen. Who really are the richest people in Croatian postwar/transition society? Where do they come from? Where does their money come from? Why them and not someone else? Are they mobsters or accidental parvenus? All these questions remain unanswered in the theatre, as well as in society.

Although a rather new profession and theatre stereotype, the Bodyguard is a far less enigmatic person: a former soldier, policeman, or heavyweight champion, with shaven head, dressed in a black suit, wearing sunglasses, a holster, and earphone, he is nothing more and nothing less than a living but mute wall between his employer and every possible threat.

One significant thing is common among some of these stereotypes—especially New Statesman, Tycoon, and Barbie: the manifest uneasiness of the body in the new apparel. Sometimes an actor keeps pulling the sleeves of his white shirt or black jacket, sometimes he twists his neck in the too-narrow collar, sometimes an actress stumbles in her too-high heels, sometimes she fights with her too-short skirt. No matter what, the enslaved body feels uneasy in the unfamiliar mode of dress. It is an old theatre routine, of course, but here it throws significant light on transition as a process not only of social transformation but of disguise as well. And disguise is, as we know, the very realm of comic theatre.

To conclude, in the last fifteen years Croatian comic theatre has been experimenting with possible sets of stereotypes organized as a new microsociety, and it has been doing so in attempts to (1) identify players of the leading roles in Croatian postwar and transition society, and (2) inform these players how to play them. Namely, the Croatian theatre has been engaged in the search for the new set of comic stereotypes not only to reflect the postwar/transition world we live in but to create and explore onstage various possible and threatening worlds and to prevent their realization by the laughter of warning.

Notes

1. Croatia: a small East European nation with fewer than five million inhabitants. After the Napoleonic Wars, the whole Croatian-populated area be-

came a partly autonomous part of the Austrian (later Austro-Hungarian) Empire. From 1918 to 1941 Croatia was a part of the Kingdom of Yugoslavia; during World War II there formally existed the Independent State of Croatia, which was practically divided between Germans and Italians, and from 1945 to 1990 Croatia was one of the six republics in the Socialist Federated Republic of Yugoslavia. Since 1992 it has been internationally recognized as an independent state. Being a border area, Croatia was for centuries the point of cultural, economic, political, and confederate conflicts and, at the same time, a point of contacts and exchanges between the East and the West; between Catholicism, Orthodoxy, and Islam; and between Romanic, Germanic, and Slavic languages and cultures.

2. Siegfried Melchinger's *Geschichte des politischen Theaters* (Frankfurt am Mein: Suhrkamp, 1974) and Jan Kott's *Shakespeare Our Contemporary* (London: Methuen, 1967) were often quoted by Croatian playwrights, actors, directors, and theatre critics throughout the 1970s and 1980s.

3. The idea of paradigmatic "social types" and their importance for the creation of adequate stock characters in theatre was developed by Croatian director Branko Gavella (1885–1962) in his book on the style of Croatian National Theatre in Zagreb *Hrvatsko glumište: Analiza nastajanja njegova stila* (Zagreb: Zora, 1953). The book has not been translated into English.

4. On "strips of behavior" and "restoration of behavior" see Richard Schechner, *Performance Studies: An Introduction,* 2nd ed. (London: Routledge, 2002), 34–36.

5. Manfred Pfister, *The Theory and Analysis of Drama* (New York: Cambridge University Press, 1991), 166.

6. See, e.g., Boris Senker, "Changes in the Croatian Theatre after 1990," *Slavic and East European Performance* 2 (1997): 32–40.

7. On "invention of tradition" as political and ideological strategy see Eric Hobsbawm and Terence Ranger, eds., *The Invention of Tradition* (New York: Cambridge University Press, 1983).

A Method to the Madness

Laughter Research, Comedy Training, and Improv

Patrick Bynane

I F THE SUREST WAY to kill a joke is to analyze it, then surely the quickest way to a deadly comic performance is to teach the actor to be "funny." Not only is such a strategy questionable, but it is most likely impossible. Simply stated, any actor training that focuses on how to be funny or deliver jokes is ultimately bound to fail. Yet anyone who has ever worked on a comedy would certainly admit that a certain, special touch is required of the actors. Painfully, many actors lack that touch and are often directed in such a way as to make achieving the required skills difficult.

These skills are different from those needed by the stand-up comic or the "serious" actor, although they are not mutually exclusive. These skills should be applicable to classical or contemporary texts, and these skills must be teachable. Traditionally, most training methods seem to be a nonsystem of either trial and error or dubious advice. How-to-be-funny books (à la the Toastmasters), vaudeville guides, imitation of favorite comic actors, and "you're-just-born-with-it" fatalism are all variations on the nonsystem theme.

The more fully realized attempts at creating a training system have historically allowed themselves to be guided by the text rather than performance. As a result many of these more developed methods end up sounding more than a bit dry and often rather absurd. Charming in its absolute certainty (and brevity) *The Craft of Comedy* by Athene Seyler and Stephen Haggard falls into this category. Writing during 1939 and 1940, Haggard and Seyler engage in an ongoing epistolary debate about the true nature of comedy and comic acting. The overall tone of the wisdom discovered by the conversation is decidedly New Critical. The text governs all; actors must discover "inner tempos," "comic rhythms," and proper syllabic emphases as though these concepts existed in some Platonic realm of comic ideals. At one point Haggard declares that "there are no two ways of saying a good line effectively—there is only the right way or the wrong way."[1] Seyler gently corrects Haggard by pointing out that with some especially well-written lines either of two ways may be equally right. After that gentle reprimand she concurs with Haggard that the "rhythm of the line" (57) should guide all comic acting choices.

"The proper balancing of a comedic sentence" and the discovery of a perfectible "comedic rhythm" certainly sound impressive and comforting to anyone who has ever flopped in a comedy. These appeals, however, to some external and absolute comic "reality" seem to deny the truly ambivalent and slippery work that is comic acting. In this essay I would like to propose not rules but suggestions or guidelines that an actor needs in order to generate a successful comic performance. These guidelines are principally derived from the work of Viola Spolin, Keith Johnstone, Paul Sills, Sanford Meisner, and Declan Donnellan, as well as from my own experiences on the stage. In no particular order of import they are (1) the ability to tell a joke without "telling a joke," (2) the ability to find fresh readings of the performance text that allow for unexpected yet effective responses and readings, (3) generosity, (4) clarity, (5) the ability to "bomb," and (6) the ability to react honestly to imaginary circumstances.

If this sounds like the basis for good acting in general, and not just in the realm of comedy, it is, more or less. I would draw your attention to the complete absence of laughter from this list. Good comic acting cannot merely be defined by laughter, causing laughter or even holding for laughter. Holding for a laugh, rather, is a technique that comes to most of us naturally as the result of what behavioral neuroscientist Robert Provine describes as "the punctuation effect."[2] This effect, in which laughter almost always occurs at the end of a phrase and almost never during a spoken phrase, "indicates that a lawful and probably neurologically based process governs the placement of laughter in speech" (ibid.). In other words, an actor doesn't hold for a laugh because he or she lacks comic training but because he or she is nervous and disregards his or her instincts. Either way, basing an acting theory on such a concept is thin soup indeed. Including laughter in a system of comedy training presupposes the certainty of getting a laugh and on a deeper structural level that comedy is essentially about producing laughter in an audience. If comedy is simply a laugh-producing discursive machine and actors simply one cog in that system, then the latest findings of laugh research hold some very grim news for future farceurs everywhere.

Although the field is still quite young and somewhat untested, laugh research has revealed some fascinating insights into the way laughter works both socially and cognitively. Part of the recent seismic shift in brain science (chemical cognitive development, bioneurology, and so forth), laugh research's leading figure is Robert R. Provine. In his 2000 book, *Laughter: A Scientific Investigation,* Provine summarizes (for a popular audience) the work and research he has conducted in the field of laughter over the past decade. Provine offers convincing evidence that laughter has very little to do with humor or the "comic spirit" but rather is an atavistic and complex neuromuscular response to specific social relationships.

Through his research Provine observes that "laughter is a social act" that plays a "non-linguistic role in social bonding, solidifying friendships and pulling people into the fold." He continues: "You can define 'friends' and 'group members' as those with whom you laugh. But laughter has a darker side, as when group members coordinate their laughter to jeer and exclude outsiders" (46–47). But the sociality of laughter reaches even deeper into our cognitive ability than how we manage our insider/outsider status among our peers. Provine has also investigated the evolutionary roots of laughter and found that chimps and other simians recognize and engage in laughter. While the chimps do not have the equivalent of social, conversational laughter, they, like humans, rarely laugh in solitary situations.[3] The social role of laughter helps, in part, to explain this. But in the work of Frans Plooij, Provine finds another cause of laughter: a need for nurturing and control. Plooij discovered that "baby chimps control the behavior of their mothers" partly and significantly through laughter.[4] Laughter through tickling or wrestling signaled mother chimps to continue play and contact with their infants. The baby chimps always initiated this behavior, usually by tugging or biting the mother. The mother chimps, however, never spontaneously engaged in this tickle play. This behavior, furthermore, has been passed on to humans. Laughter is one of the earliest signals by which a human infant signals a desire for more contact.[5]

Further undermining the assumed relationship between comedy and laughter, Provine has found that most laughter occurs after entirely commonplace phrases and utterances. As he observes, "Most prelaugh dialogue is like that of an interminable television situation comedy scripted by an extremely ungifted writer. When we hear peals of laughter at social gatherings, we are not experiencing the results of a furious rate of joke telling. The next time you are around laughing people, examine for yourself the general witlessness of prelaugh comments" (42).

Also, in surveying prelaugh comments and the laugh incidents they produced, Provine found that females are the leading laughers, and males are the foremost laugh producers (28). Typical lines that produced laughter were such witty observations as "I'll see you guys later," "We can handle this," "I told you so," "How are you?" and "I know" (40–41). Molière has little to fear. Laughter in most cases functions as conversational punctuation, a sign of dominance, a sign of submissiveness, a signal of agreement, and/or a way of forming or reinforcing a bond but rarely as a product of humor. If we conceive of comedy as simply about producing laughter and if we take Provine's research and apply it to producing comedy, then we should forget about training actors in anything that even resembles a comic "style" and simply cast our comedies with men and fill our audiences with sympathetic women. Or we could just tickle our audiences, but that's another essay.

Interestingly and, perhaps, counterintuitively, Provine's research potentially imparts some scientific muscle to contemporary, poststructuralist literary theory as well. If poststructuralism has taught us anything, it is that meaning is slippery at best. Language is but one code in a frayed tapestry of codes. Identifying "laughter from comedy" as a discursive fact seems the ultimate rejection of everything poststructuralism might teach us about theatre practice. Attempting to control the laughter of the audience by "being funny" or through "comic acting" means to place the actor in a position of total interpretive control. The actor is not just defining all language but is even going so far as to assume control over the mysterious neuromuscular process we call "laughing." In this situation the actor is forcing one meaning over all others. No matter what your definition of *acting, comedy,* or *theatre* may be (or your feelings regarding contemporary, poststructuralist thinking), I think we can all agree that forcing onstage is failure.

The point of this very brief survey of laughter is that producing laughter is a less than useful way to define comedy and, also, spectacularly unreliable. Any method of training actors for comedy or any notion of comedy that holds the generating of laughter as primary and immanent is incomplete at best and bound to fail at worst. Therefore comedy and comic acting must strive for something else. Perhaps comedy is a unique relationship between characters within the text and actors manifesting characters onstage. This special relationship creates a similarly unique relationship between the audience, actors, characters, and text. Be that as it may, comedy and comic acting must reach for something different from simple laughter.

Viola Spolin intuited this when she wrote *Improvisation for the The-atre* and offered a philosophy of actor training not grounded in text-bound interpretation or in controlling meaning but a method rooted in relationships and responsive action. Or, as Spolin more succinctly writes, "Without the other player, there is no game. We cannot play tag if there is no one to tag."[6] In moving toward an understanding of actor train-ing fixed in relational communication processes and not in specific tech-niques, Spolin challenges the very notion that an actor can be trained for something so specific (and yet virtually indefinable) as comedy. As she observes, "When a theater technique or stage convention is regarded as a ritual and the reason for its inclusion in the list of actors' skills is lost, it is useless. An artificial barrier is set up when techniques are separated from direct experiencing. No one separates batting a ball from the game itself" (14).

I offer here six guidelines for comic training. These are not rules or techniques to be mastered but underlying structures that might steer ac-tors to that sense of experience, response, game playing, and awareness needed on the comic stage.

There may be nothing so miserable as watching the office or class clown try his or her hand at stand-up. The jokes bomb, the punch lines are telegraphed from miles away, and the desperation and forcing grow exponentially after each failed attempt. Much the same thing happens when actors are instructed to give the punch line that final boost or "button" to signal the arrival of humor. And much like our hypothetical stand-up flop, an actor who does this destroys the trust between actor and audience and actor and actor. The comic actor must be able to let the joke happen within the context of the performance. By the time the live performance occurs, it is too late to really change much anyway. "Punching up" a line or telegraphing the joke won't and can't help. Concurrent to this guideline is developing the ability to "bomb." Even the most experienced actors can get caught up in a seemingly "surefire" comic moment that fails. Strong comic acting depends on the ability to leave the past behind and focus on the present moment. Wallowing in a lost comic opportunity or, even worse, trying to resurrect or save that lost comic opportunity should be trained out of all actors.

Comedy lives on freshness and immediacy. A comic performance that attempts to recreate the exact intention and context that inspired the au-thor or original creator of a comic moment will feel "stale." Dogberry can only be funny for a contemporary audience if the actor playing Dog-berry finds the reading of Dogberry that speaks to today's episteme. At-tempting to recreate Wil Kempe's performance, obviously, is bound to fail. Recreating Michael Keaton's performance would be absolutely disastrous. Finding such a reading of a role or a moment must come from the production's special language discovered in rehearsal and through the unique, trusting interaction of the assembled cast and production crew. An actor falling back on other readings is usually feeling anxiety or a negative urgency about his or her surroundings. As Spolin notes, "Any player who feels urgent about the game and plays it alone does not trust his fellow players" (45).

Strong comic acting depends on taking from what exists in the context of the production, but it depends even more on giving. Great comic actors know how to pull back, give focus, regain focus, and act on the environment that surrounds him or her. Great comic acting never depends on "hamming it up" or scene stealing. "Any player who 'steals' a scene," says Spolin, "is a thief" (45). Generosity means not just giving focus or active response but honesty: honesty about what is really going on in a production at a given moment and honesty about the role an actor is playing within a larger structure. Generosity in comic acting means recognizing that no one person can carry an entire scene, much less an entire play; attempting to do so leads to blocking and negation. Keith Johnstone rightly observes, "Blocking is a form of aggression."[7] Ironically, many financially successful comic actors have developed blocking into a highly developed skill; great comic actors rely on generous action.

Comedy may seem to be a world of chaos and disorder. Any comic performance that depends on such bedlam, however, quickly finds a level of anarchy that is no longer comic but depressing and a little scary. Direct and clear action and purpose (in short, clarity) must guide all of the actor's movements and choices. Screwball comedy "works" not just because of its speed but because governing the speed are clear and direct choices and motivations. The tragic has room built into it for ambivalence and ambiguity; comedy does not. Muddled choices, muddled words, and muddled motivations have never been a part of comic acting, regardless of one's definition of comedy.

Sanford Meisner once defined acting as the ability to react honestly to imaginary circumstances. The notion of the "honest reaction" may be the single most difficult skill for an actor to develop. An audience can practically smell a false or pre-scripted reaction. Like forcing a joke or telegraphing a punch line, reacting dishonestly, or to something that the actor wishes were present, further breaks down the integral relationships that comic acting depends on. Spolin defines the dynamic is this way: "Unless needed to solve a specific problem in a play, remembered experiences (recalls) are avoided as the group works for immediate (right now) spontaneous ones. Every individual has enough muscular memory and stored-away experience that can be used in a present-time situation without deliberately abstracting it from the total organism."[8] Declan Donnellan uses the term *targets* to make much the same point. Either way, the appearance of spontaneity on which comedy depends can only happen through honest reactions.

Simply sketching a handful of guidelines hardly makes for an actor training system. The real difficulty appears when a pedagogical methodology must be devised. Obviously, just throwing inexperienced actors in front of an audience and telling them to be funny lacks a certain usefulness and efficacy, not to mention compassion. Unfortunately, on the university level we seem to do this quite regularly. Not only are valuable opportunities for instruction and development lost by doing this but many self-defeating skills are reinforced. What is needed is a form that teaches responsiveness, clarity, and adaptability while developing the ability to form generous, creative relationships that serve the performance.

I propose that the teaching philosophies and methods of Viola Spolin, Keith Johnstone, and Paul Sills (in other words, improv) serve this purpose in a way that is simply more efficacious and more successful than other processes. Perhaps most important, this methodology starts from the somewhat radical premise that acting can, in fact, be taught and that this journey should be pleasurable. Spolin writes in her introduction to *Improvisation for the Theatre,* "Acting can be taught to the 'average' as well as the 'talented' if the teaching process is oriented towards making the theatre techniques so intuitive that they become the students' own" (4). For Spolin as for Johnstone this means a series of games through which the actors' intuitive sense of play and playfulness are teased out and made apparent. This requires some fairly significant shifts in the teacher-student relationship. Johnstone reminds his readers that a teacher of improv cannot be afraid of giving "I am playing" signals to their students. Doing so, Johnstone offers, would make the work of actor training and improv pleasurable and, most important, accessible.[9]

Such a shift also means challenging authority and authoritarianism. In one of her more provocative passages Spolin warns:

> The language and attitudes of authoritarianism must be constantly scourged if the total personality is to emerge as a working unit. All words which shut doors, have emotional content or implication, attack the student-actor's personality, or keep a student slavishly dependent on a teacher's judgment are to be avoided. Since most of us were brought up by the approval/disapproval method, constant self-surveillance is necessary on the part of the teacher-director to eradicate it in himself so that it will not en-

ter the teacher-student relationship. The expectancy of judgment prevents free relationships within the acting workshops. (8)

Johnstone phrases this challenge in another way: "I'm teaching spontaneity, and therefore I tell them that they mustn't try to control the future, or to win; and that they're to have an empty head and just watch. When it's their turn to take part they're to come out and just do what they're asked to, and *see what happens*. It's this decision not to try and control the future which allows the students to be spontaneous."[10] To shake students and young actors out of their torpor, we must give them the tools to negotiate a deeply internalized authoritarianism and embrace creative spontaneity.

One possible approach to creating such a training program might proceed thus: a two-semester cycle of training that begins with the most basic awareness exercises found in the traditional improv texts. From these games the class could move to audience-suggested scenes. Throughout, the teacher-director must assertively side-coach and keep the students focused on the objectives of the game or exercise; attempts to be funny or make jokes end the scene or game. Going for a joke or trying to control the game through stealing or other related tactics reasserts the authoritarianism that must be challenged and confronted for this system to work. At the end of the first semester the actor-students should publicly present their work. It is important to remind and reinforce the fundamental role the audience plays in the whole process.

The second semester could begin with more advanced games and exercises, including group-scripted scenes. Eventually the improv games should give way to text-based comic scenes. Side-coaching should not disappear, however. The teacher-director will still be needed to keep the actors focused on the target or objective of their character within the "rules" of the scene. Once again, this semester should end with public performances of text-based scenes that have become central to the class. The more chances the actor-students have to experience a successful comic scene (not one that gets big laughs but one that accomplishes the objectives of the relationships in the scene), the more their skills will develop. The deeper they grasp the notion that comedy cannot simply be about producing laughter but can only be found in directness and honesty, the more skilled they will become as accomplished comic actors.

Wrestling with these issues and attempting to devise a system of comic training is important because comic acting is a skill that can be taught; people are not born funny. Some of our greatest comic actors have been downright depressing and miserable individuals. Furthermore, comedy may be the most unforgiving of genres. Serious drama, tragedy, and melodrama all can withstand a few egregious moments of self-indulgence (method acting anyone?), but such behavior is, bluntly stated, the death of comic acting. An improvisational course of training that follows the precepts of the above mentioned authors and teachers will not teach comedy or "funniness." To do so would be contradictory to their stated goals and aesthetic philosophies. Furthermore, as the new field of laugh research suggests, it would be absurd and highly counterintuitive. However, an improvisational course of actor training will teach relationship, playfulness, connection, and active listening. Timing, clarity, and honest reaction come directly from such lessons. These, ultimately, are the required skills of a successful comic actor.

Notes

1. Athene Seyler and Stephen Haggard, *The Craft of Comedy* (New York: Theatre Arts Books, 1957), 54.

2. Robert R. Provine, *Laughter: A Scientific Investigation* (New York: Penguin, 2001), 37.

3. Ibid., 92.

4. Ibid., 93.

5. Ibid.

6. Viola Spolin, *Improvisation for the Theatre* (Evanston, IL: Northwestern University Press, 1963), 46.

7. Keith Johnstone, *Impro: Improvisation and the Theatre* (New York: Routledge, 1981), 94.

8. Spolin, *Improvisation for the Theatre,* 40.

9. Johnstone, *Impro,* 32.

10. Ibid.

Comedy Tonight . . . and Tomorrow

A Funny Thing Happened on the Way to the Forum and Laughter through the Ages

Diana Calderazzo

LAUGHTER, IT SEEMS, is a timeless activity that has served to unify theatrical audiences since the era of the ancient Greeks and Romans; and research has indicated that the activity of laughing in which contemporary audiences engage is much the same as that experienced by ancient audiences. Furthermore, not only has the process of engaging in laughter in response to the theatrical event changed very little during the past twenty-five hundred years, but many of the basic situations and stock characters traditionally associated with humor have survived equally as long. From the comedies of Terence and Plautus to the scenarios of the commedia dell'arte troupes to the sketches of the burlesque and vaudeville stages, theatre through the ages has encouraged audiences to laugh at dueling brothers, doting lovers, and clowning comics.

Contemporary theatrical pieces continue, of course, to draw on the classic comic tradition, perhaps none with such blatant aplomb as Stephen Sondheim, Burt Shevelove, and Larry Gelbart's *A Funny Thing Happened on the Way to the Forum,* featured for the first time on Broadway in 1962.[1] During its successful first run, *Forum* reincarnated the ancient Roman farcical style of Plautus, recalling the historical evolution of comedy in the process and successfully encouraging contemporary spectators to engage in such farcical antics as have amused historical audiences for centuries.

While it is widely agreed that these comic elements continue to elicit laughter, the cognitive basis of this laughter is not as widely observed. Cognitively, laughter relies on both biological process and environmental context. Thus, in reaction to a piece such as *Forum,* audience laughter emanates from both a universal response and a reaction to social and cultural elements that have evolved through the ages. Drawing on the research of such cognitive scientists as Jaak Panksepp, Antonio Damasio, Robert Latta, Robert R. Provine, and others,[2] I will endeavor to offer a basic explanation of this response in terms of audience behavior ensuing from those elements of *Forum* that have, through the ages, earned the reputation of being "funny." This will require establishing a brief, but focused, foundation highlighting some of the main points regarding the nature of laughter and its relationship to emotional engagement in cognitive terms before moving on to analyze the emotional participation of audience members in response to particular elements within *Forum*. Utilizing this cognitive basis, I will argue that through an invitation to emotional engagement, the humorous elements of *Forum* offer its audiences both biological and environmental stimulants to laughter.

First, according to several cognitive scientists, the activity of laughter works on a basic level as an indicator of emotional engagement. From Panksepp's perspective, laughter is closely related to human engagement in "PLAY," a term Panksepp and his research partner, Luc Ciompi, use to describe not simply an activity but a complex "emotional system."[3] Panksepp states that "the hallmark for PLAY circuitry in action for humans is laughter," and "laughter . . . may emerge from PLAY motivation."[4] Thus, when human beings engage in the emotional system of PLAY, laughter often results. Though Panksepp's definition of *PLAY* is wide-ranging and complex, he makes it clear that higher levels of PLAY may involve theatrical playing, appealing to participants on a "dramatic/symbolic" level.[5] The potential for PLAY, then, around which laughter is shown to function, appears to abound within the environment of the theatrical event.

Second, engagement in emotional systems (such as Panksepp's notion of PLAY) is necessary for the healthy and balanced maintenance of the human life form. Damasio defines this function of emotional engagement as "part and parcel of the regulation we call homeostasis." "Homeostasis," Damasio explains, "refers to the coordinated and largely automated physiological reactions required to maintain steady internal states in a living organism."[6] Thus, PLAY and other forms of emotional engagement appear to be necessary to maintaining human health and are thus part of the biological processes essential to our basic interaction with the world around us. If this is the case, and if, as indicated above, PLAY leads to laughter, it follows that laughter may be one indicator of a balanced, healthy biological system. Serving to indicate such a basic internal function, laughter, then, appears to be an innate, biological reaction common to all human beings, a conclusion supported by the research of Panksepp, who asserts that "laughter is not learned by imitation, since blind and deaf children laugh readily."[7]

Finally, although cognitive scientists argue that the *mechanism* of human laughter is innate, they also assert that the *tendency to engage* in laughter may be learned and does, in fact, lend itself to being communicated from one human being to another. Robert R. Provine observes this contagious nature of laughter in his analysis of the phenomena of laugh epidemics, "holy" laughter, and laugh tracks.[8] One example, on which Provine elaborates in a fair amount of detail, describes a laugh epidemic that occurred in 1962 in a Tanzanian village, causing debilitating laughter in more than one hundred students and requiring their school to be shut down for two months.[9]

Thus, cognitive studies on the origins of laughter indicate that laughter is (1) closely related to the emotional system of PLAY, (2) the result of a biological tendency to maintain balance in the human organism, and (3) contagious. These three biological aspects of laughter suggest why laughter has remained a common human response to life situations, including the theatrical event, through the ages. In particular, however, these observations serve to launch a discussion of why specific theatrical events, such as the performance of *A Funny Thing Happened on the Way to the Forum*, might elicit laughter as a biological response.

Forum presents to its audience members a direct and ongoing invitation to engage in the basic emotional system of dramatic/symbolic PLAY. From the opening moment, when Prologus takes the stage to announce, "Playgoers, I bid you welcome," to the final syllables of the cast reminder to the audience that they have just witnessed a "comedy tonight," the show maintains its status as an evening (or afternoon) of PLAY. Indeed, the actors clearly indicate to audience members that they are putting on a show—much like children engaging in PLAY, who, according to Panksepp, "like to stage various skits and shows, but as they attempt to perform seriously, all too often they simply end up giggling in glee."[10] Though the actors in *Forum* (hopefully) do not conclude the show by simply resorting to the giggles, they do establish through Sondheim's brilliant list of comedic elements to be presented, their intent to laugh at themselves by commenting every so often on the humorous nature of their own presentation. And since laughter is contagious, *Forum* in this way invites its audiences into a humorous PLAY world in which actors and audience members alike may become engaged.

Another aspect of *Forum* serving to invite its audiences to engage in the biological function of laughter is related to a noted tendency of laughter to signal the maintenance of homeostasis. The cognitive theorist Robert L. Latta describes the process of laughter in terms of its allowance of a "cognitive shift" that in the most basic sense effectively brings the human organism from an "un-relaxed" state to a "relaxed" state.[11] Latta thus recalls Damasio's more general description of the maintenance of homeostasis as a reaction that serves to maintain steady internal states with the human organism. According to Latta, stories of events that stimulate laughter do so because they present to their participants situations that describe and cause a state of nonrelaxation, only to result in a situation that somehow allows a shift in cognitive process, restoring in its participants the feeling of relaxation. He cites, as an example of such a story, Woody Allen's narrative "No *Kaddish* for Weinstein": "Weinstein lay under the covers, staring at the ceiling in a depressed torpor. Outside, sheets of humid air rose from the pavement in stifling waves. The sound of traffic was deafening at this hour, and in addition to all this, his bed was on fire."[12]

Latta tells us that "the initial portion of Weinstein's situation is to be taken straight. But of course the final clause, 'his bed was on fire,' is not" (ibid.). The "straight" portion of the story, describing Weinstein's surroundings, produces tension and suspense, an "un-relaxed" feeling, in Latta's participants or in audience members. The moment, however, that audiences are introduced to the unrealistic aspect of the man lying pensively in a burning bed, they engage in a "cognitive shift" that changes the premise of the story from realistic to unrealistic, from "straight" to humorous. Congruently, they are able to move from the unrelaxed state provoked by the premise to a relaxed state allowed by the cognitive shift resulting from the final statement.

A similar process occurs when spectators who are engaged in the story presented through a theatrical event laugh following the delivery of a punch line. Consider the scene in act I of *Forum* when Pseudolus obtains Hysterium's book of potions and devises a plan to utilize a sleeping potion as a means to unite Philia with Hero, consequently obtaining his freedom:

> His book of potions! And my pass to freedom! What I need is his sleeping potion. With a drop or two of that the breath stops short, the eyes slam shut, the body hangs limp. I shall mix a few drops in a beaker of wine and give it to the girl to drink. I show Lycus that she has died of the plague and tell Hero to dispose of the body. Then they to the boat, I to the hills, *(Points to the audience.)* and you to your homes. *(Looks through the pages, then:)* I just remembered something frightening. I cannot read![13]

According to Latta's formula, the first eight sentences above set up the joke, working to build tension resulting in the unrelaxed state in the spectator as Pseudolus constructs his plan. Audience members know that, although his plan is without a doubt far-fetched, its execution is not out of the question given the farcical nature of the piece; and they follow his thought process with as much earnestness as is possible under the circumstances. Pseudolus then builds tension to a climax with his line, "I just remembered something frightening," only to release that tension and return his audiences to a more relaxed state resulting in laughter with the line "I cannot read." In Latta's terms this final brief observation serves as the punch line, producing the cognitive shift. Like the image of the bed on fire in the earlier example, the image of an illiterate Pseudolus establishes a change in the situation constructed within the setup (that of a brilliant Pseudolus fabricating a master plan). The resulting release of tension promotes relaxation and, consequently, laughter in the spectator. Jokes such as this one occur throughout Shevelove and Gelbart's script, as well as within Sondheim's lyrics, resulting in a continual accumulation and release of tension within the spectator causing a shift from unrelaxation to relaxation and stimulating laughter in response.

Laughter, then, through its cognitive association with the emotional system of PLAY, its tendency to reflect the maintenance of homeostatic balance, and its contagious nature, appears to function on a biological level as a consequence of audience engagement in specific elements of *Forum*. Yet scientists observe that cognitive processes function socially, as well as biologically, and the process of laughter is no exception. Both Panksepp's and Provine's studies address the function of laughter as an indicator of social relationships that are environmentally defined, referring to the evolution of the laughter function based on its ability to, in Panksepp's terms, "signal to others one's social mood and sense of camaraderie."[14] In social situations, then, laughter is often the result of the establishment of specific relationships that are determined within their environment to be humorous.

One of the most common social relationships shown to induce laughter is that which exploits a power dynamic, as Panksepp explains: "Laughter may now be one signal for victory within playful social encounters as the philosopher Thomas Hobbes argues, just as being in the top position during pinning in RAT [Rough and Tumble] play is the preferred physical position" (ibid.). Within the boundaries of the emotional system of PLAY, then, humans appear to possess a tendency to "make fun of," or laugh at, those whom they consider inferior.

Provine agrees, emphasizing the human tendency to laugh at those we may classify as odd and arguing that this type of laughter feeds the human inclination to maintain social hierarchies.[15] Given *Forum*'s tendency to invite its audiences to look on its featured characters as misfits, the show offers much potential for the stimulation of laughter in this respect. Indeed, *Forum* not only features such odd characters but advertises them, promising in its opening number to deliver "lovers, liars, and clowns"; "courtesans and eunuchs"; "panderers"; "philanderers"; and other enticingly strange figures. In addition, based on Panksepp's observations, audience members are likely to be amused not only by the existence of such "funny" characters onstage but also by the nature of their interactions: "Laughter . . . often occurs in response to seeing others hurt, humiliated, or embarrassed, and it indicates a recognition of the victim's slapstick predicament coupled with the feeling that one has been psychologically luckier and perhaps even smarter than the poor sod who is the brunt of some misfortune."[16] "Slapstick predicaments" and "poor sods," of course, form much of the premise of *Forum*, and when presented in the context of the emotional system of PLAY as described above, they elicit unabashed laughter from spectators who are able to release tension through their perception of dramatic characters displaying socially interactive power dynamics exaggerated to the point of ridiculousness.

Socially influenced cognitive processes shown to initiate laughter may be language-based as well. According to Panksepp, "It must also be noted that playfulness in humans can eventually be expressed in symbolic ways, which may be largely linguistic, such as puns, joking, and verbal jibes, that lead to a great deal of mirth and laughter" (283). Such puns and verbal jokes, which may be said to demonstrate "salient meanings," abound within the PLAY atmosphere described above. Salient meanings, researched in detail by psycholinguist Rachel Giora, may be understood in simple terms to describe multiple levels of denotation resulting when at least two separate but parallel decoding processes occur in the brain. Giora's example illustrates a pun: "Two men walk into a bar and the third man ducks."[17] Regarding the single word *bar*, a simple parallel interpretation originates from two sources: "mental lexicon" [the common mental image of two men walking into a tavern to have a drink] and "contextual information" [the reference to one man ducking to avoid a long pole] (ibid., 37). As in the setup and punch-line example discussed earlier, two separate approaches are offered for understanding the information presented. As we have seen, such multiple approaches lead to a release of tension often resulting in laughter, as likely happened in response to the following scene late in act 1 in *Forum*, when Miles Gloriosus makes his first entrance, accompanied by his marching soldiers:

SOLDIERS. One, two, one, two . . .
MILES. We not only fought but we won, too!
SOLDIERS. One, two, one, two . . . Left, right, left, right . . .
MILES. There's none of the enemy left, right?
SOLDIERS. Right! Left! . . . uh . . . Ri-uh-left!
(Utter confusion.)[18]

The salient meanings suggested by the words *one, two* versus *won, too* and *left, right* versus *left, right?* predictably cause the "utter confusion" that results, as well as an accompanying tension release leading to the urge to laugh in the average spectator.

Another, more complex, manifestation of salient meanings as Giora describes them is irony, which tends to originate from more culturally based than social- or language-based traditions. For example, audiences may be conditioned to expect particular scenarios based on the setup of a culturally established, age-old comic tradition, while experiencing a show such as *Forum;* yet their expectations may in specific instances describe the exact opposite of what is presented. In Giora's analytical construct this phenomenon may fall under the heading of "echoic irony," in which the attitude ultimately expressed is the opposite of the opinion first echoed, resulting in the expression of thwarted expectations, as in the following example: "Gus just graduated from high school and he didn't know what to do. One day he saw an ad about the Navy. It said that the Navy was not just a job, but an adventure. So Gus joined up. Soon he was aboard a ship doing all sorts of boring things. One day as he was peeling potatoes he said to his buddy, 'This sure is an exciting life.'"[19] The sarcasm Gus expresses in his comment to his buddy, as Giora explains, demonstrates echoic irony only because expectations of "not just a job, but an adventure" had been previously established, while the reality of the situation proved to describe the opposite scenario.

Similarly, the commedia tradition of stock characters has taught spectators through the ages to expect characters with certain names or affiliations to behave in specific, predetermined ways. (For example, the miser character type should consider money to be sacred, the young lover should be properly doting and fantasizing, and the hero should of course be heroic.) The behavior of certain characters in *Forum,* however, often undermines this tradition—Hero must rely on his slave to win the woman he loves, Miles Gloriosus is glorious only in his own eyes, and a slave named Hysterium sings a song entitled "I'm Calm." In this sense echoic irony presents situations opposite to those originally set up and expected by audience members. While these examples are more situational than the punch-line-based joke described above in Latta's description of the process of laughter, the function of cognitive shift from one perceptive approach to another appears to be present, indicating a potential to elicit laughter here as well.

As indicated by the above discussion, audience expectations often exert substantial influence on spectators' ultimate reactions to a performance. Cognitive film theorist Edward Branigan clarifies this phenomenon, explaining that audiences evaluate a performance by "constructing large-scale, hierarchical patterns which represent a particular story as an abstract grouping of knowledge based on an underlying schema."[20] Branigan's analysis is complex, but, in basic terms, he explains that audiences form impressions of the performance event they are experiencing based both on images presented to them in the moment and on organized groups of images (schemata) formed from memory and previous knowledge of other theatrical events. Thus, when audiences attend a farce such as *Forum,* they tend to arrive at the theatre with predetermined schemata in place, describing their expectations based on their varying awareness regarding the genre. At the very least, they are likely to know that the production will be funny and will feature a happy ending, and most will expect to experience stock characters, dynamic physical routines, and plenty of verbal antics and jokes such as those already discussed. As *Forum* in 1962 was a theatrical event steeped in comic tradition, it carried much potential either to successfully fulfill audience expectations as determined by spectators' previously constructed concepts of comedy or simply to flop as a reconstruction of the significant elements historically associated with the comic tradition. Thus, whether or not *Forum* "worked" in this sense was influenced at least in part by the manner in which each of the biological, social, and cultural elements discussed above as primary to the invocation of laughter actually delivered to audiences what it promised within the context of the comic tradition.

Fortunately, *Forum* succeeded in this respect, never backing down from its goal to boldly provide undiluted farce to its audiences and strictly adhering to the ancient comic tradition it mimicked in a time when musicals were often expected to be romantic and plays were often expected to deliver at least some degree of social significance. Indeed, Burt Shevelove and Larry Gelbart, collaborating on the libretto in 1958, emphasized their goal of maintaining a level of truth to the original approach utilized by Plautus in such works as *Pseudolus* and *Casina.* Gelbart's biographer, Jay Malarcher, quotes the writer as follows: "We would preserve the classic unities of time, place, and action. We would use the classic characters of Plautus. We would have no anachronisms or sly references to today."[21]

Thus, from the show's conception, *Forum*'s writers smartly worked to create a piece that would follow through on its billing as pure farce and remain uncomplicated by contemporary annotations. Accordingly, they included the above-mentioned prologue, which served to set the stage for the ensuing antics; and they featured the stock characters of the innocent lovers, Hero and Philia, and the money-hungry Lycus, reminiscent of the merchant Pantalone in commedia, as well as many others. All served on the most basic level to appeal to spectators' innate sense of fun, as well as their conceptual and cultural understanding of what constitutes humor, prompting reviewers such as Robert Coleman to appreciate the show, simply seeing it as "a burlesque on the plays of Plautus" and happily stating, "You won't find anything more hilarious the length of Broadway."[22] Coleman's reference to burlesque, which of course took on its own identity as a comedic art form during the first quarter of the twentieth century, illustrates his vision of *Forum* as a successful salute to the comic tradition.

Furthermore, *Forum*'s out-of-town tryouts served to argue for the power of audience expectations in determining their ultimate judgment of the theatrical event by evaluating its authenticity as a farce. Sondheim biographer Meryle Secrest explains that the composer had written a song called "Love Is in the Air" to serve as the opening song within the show's prologue. (The director, George Abbott, had rejected his first composition, entitled "Invocation.") "Love Is in the Air," however, did not work within the prologue because, as collaborator Jerome Robbins explained, "The opening number is killing the show. You open with a charming number and the audience does not know what they're in for, that it's a real farce. You've got to write an opening number that says baggy pants."[23] In response Sondheim composed "Comedy Tonight," which of course remained true to the vision of the piece. Robbins's phrase "a true farce" formed the key to explaining audience expectations—the show was billed as a farce, and audiences needed to be assured early on that it was not a reference to farce, a questioning of farce, or a parody of farce, but it was indeed the real thing. As such, it allowed its audiences permission to laugh without reserve, and critics expressed their hearty appreciation of the classic comedy presented.

Walter Kerr, for example, reviewing the show on its opening night, observed that "this [musical] is very classical. You know that from the moment that Zero Mostel first appears in front of a noble red curtain, obviously stained with tears of a thousand tragedians, to raise his quivering hand high in the air, lift his Roman brow to a point where the man in the spotlight booth can hit it properly, and to welcome us all to the halls of Thespis as though we hadn't been there since Walter Hampden's last road company came back in."[24]

Kerr identified with every bit of comedic nostalgia *Forum* offered. Similarly, Howard Taubman, in his review of *Forum,* noted enjoyable parallels between that musical and the comic traditions of ancient Rome, burlesque, vaudeville, and the routines of the Marx Brothers. "Nothing really happens that isn't older than the forum, more ancient than the agoras in Athens," he concluded. "But somehow you keep laughing as if the old sight and sound gags were as good as new."[25] Richard Watts Jr. concurred, appearing almost guilty for enjoying a seemingly outdated tradition: "It is simply a burlesque show, with a pseudo-classic Roman setting and a firm conviction that pace and simple basic humor are important to farce. But the fact remains that, in its shameless fashion, it is downright hilarious."[26]

Finally, *Forum*'s significance as a true farce was heightened by its assumed role of offering to its audiences a refreshing alternative to the romantic musicals that preceded it on Broadway. Longtime *Variety* critic Hobe Morrison astutely observed this aspect of *Forum*: "the show is, in essence, a gigantic spoof of traditional musical comedy. . . . For example, a ballad titled 'Lovely' is a travesty of romantic tunes in general and the *West Side Story* song hit 'I'm Pretty' ['I Feel Pretty'], in particular. By no coincidence," Morrison observes, "Sondheim wrote the lyrics for *West Side Story* and both words and music for *A Funny Thing*."[27] Morrison praised the show's tendency not only to present historical forms of comedy but also to comment on then-current trends of musical comedy in America, which in 1962 owed much to the romantic book musicals of Leonard Bernstein and others, including Sondheim's mentor, Oscar Hammerstein II, and his writing partner Richard Rodgers. As writer Burt Shevelove noted, "There were plenty of touching, even tragic, lovers, plenty of dream ballets, and plenty of important truths, stated and restated, but no fun."[28]

One role of *Forum* in 1962, then, was to provide the "fun" that some argued was missing from contemporary musical comedy by good-naturedly pointing to the romantic clichés of the musical comedies of the previous decade and by reminding audiences of their comic roots in the less subtle forms of New Comedy, commedia, and vaudeville. To the effect that *Forum* provided a response to what could be seen as the overpopularized genre of the romantic musical comedy, it elicited the following praise from Robert Brustein: "[Farce and slapstick] have not quite disappeared, because a raucous farce just breezed into town bringing with it the atmosphere of balmier days. *A Funny Thing Happened on the Way to the Forum,* to be sure has to be smuggled in disguised as a 'musical' in order to be produced at all; but the disguise is so transparent that none but the charity audiences will be deceived."[29] Brustein was, of course, applauding the freshness of *Forum*'s return to the classical tradition.

A Funny Thing Happened on the Way to the Forum in 1962—running 964 performances, winning six Tony Awards, and boasting two Broadway revivals—worked on universal, as well as environmentally specific, levels to appeal to its audiences' senses of humor. Calling on spectators' universal capacity for laughter, Sondheim, Shevelove, and Gelbart invited audiences to engage in an environment of PLAY based in their expectations of ancient farce. Once emotionally engaged, spectators could release tension through laughter in response to humorous inconsistencies established by punch lines, salient meanings, character inconsistencies, social misfits, and other cognitive phenomena. In addition, from a cultural perspective, *Forum* successfully elicited laughter by wholeheartedly reincarnating a classical tradition that also reintroduced its 1962 audiences to a form of comedy on the musical theatre stage to which they were not accustomed at the time—truly offering comedy to its audiences in the form of "something familiar" as well as "something peculiar."

Notes

1. The show was revived in 1972 and again in 1996; the film version was released in 1966.

2. I wish to thank Bruce McConachie at the University of Pittsburgh for leading me to these sources and whose forthcoming book on audience spectating provides the inspiration for this essay.

3. Luc Ciompi and Jaak Panksepp, "Energetic Effects of Emotions on Cognitions: Complementary Psychobiological and Psychosocial Findings," in *Consciousness and Emotion: Agency, Conscious Choice, and Selective Perception,* ed. Ralph D. Ellis and Natika Newton (Amsterdam: John Benjamins Publishing, 2005), 23–56.

4. Jaak Panksepp, *Affective Neuroscience* (New York: Oxford University Press, 1998), 287. Panksepp's full discussion of the relationship between play and laughter can be found on pages 287–89.

5. Ibid., 283.

6. Antonio Damasio, *The Feeling of What Happens: Body and Emotion in the Making of Consciousness* (New York: Harcourt Brace, 1999), 39–40.

7. Panksepp, *Affective Neuroscience,* 287.

8. Robert R. Provine, *Laughter: A Scientific Investigation* (New York: Viking, 2000), 129–51. Because of laughter's relationship to emotional engagement, the contagious nature of laughter can also be attributed to "emotional contagion," a term coined by the cognitive scientist Robert M. Gordon to describe the "catchy" nature of emotions.

9. Ibid., 130.

10. Panksepp, *Affective Neuroscience*, 283.

11. Robert L. Latta, *The Basic Humor Process: A Cognitive Shift Theory and a Case against Incongruity* (Berlin: Mouton de Gruyter, 1999).

12. Ibid., 82.

13. Burt Shevelove, Larry Gelbart, and Stephen Sondheim, *A Funny Thing Happened on the Way to the Forum* (New York: Dodd, Mead, 1962), 49–50.

14. Panksepp, *Affective Neuroscience*, 287.

15. Provine, *Laughter*, 15–20.

16. Panksepp, *Affective Neuroscience*, 287.

17. Rachel Giora, *On Our Mind: Salience, Context, and Figurative Language* (New York: Oxford University Press, 2003), 37–38.

18. Shevelove, Gelbart, and Sondheim, *A Funny Thing Happened on the Way to the Forum*, 73.

19. Giora, *On Our Mind*, 64.

20. Edward Branigan, *Narrative Comprehension and Film* (London: Routledge, 1992), 16.

21. Jay Malarcher, *The Classically American Comedy of Larry Gelbart* (Lanham, MD: Scarecrow, 2003), 60.

22. Robert Coleman, "Funny Things Are Happening at Alvin," *New York Mirror*, May 9, 1962.

23. Meryle Secrest, *Sondheim: A Life* (New York: Knopf, 1998), 154.

24. Walter Kerr, "First Night Report: 'A Funny Thing . . . ,'" *New York Herald Tribune*, May 9, 1962.

25. Howard Taubman, "Theatre: 'A Funny Thing Happened . . . ,'" *New York Times*, May 9, 1962.

26. Richard Watts Jr., "Riotous Life of the Old Romans," *New York Post*, May 9, 1962.

27. Hobe Morrison, "Show on Broadway: *A Funny Thing Happened on the Way to the Forum*, " *Variety*, May 16, 1962.

28. Quoted in Malarcher, *The Classically American Comedy of Larry Gelbart*, 58.

29. Robert Brustein, "Vox Populi, Vox Box," *New Republic*, May 28, 1962, 29.

Performing Molière's Comedies

Challenges and Approaches

Biliana Stoytcheva-Horissian

Comedy has no limits.
    —Don Richardson, *Acting without Agony*

COMEDY HAS a long history before and after Jean-Baptiste Poquelin—later known as Molière—began exploring his dramatic ability, but time has proven the ageless quality, critical power, and contemporary sound of his works. Molière defied time, space, and language boundaries, and his comedies have survived changes of style, society, and taste, becoming icons of comic writing.

This essay offers four separate approaches for handling common stumbling blocks in performing Molière. I have selected *The School for Wives*,[1] Molière's first great verse comedy, to demonstrate suggested methods and techniques when needed. The play offers possibilities for a wide range of interpretations. In a unique way it balances the extremely physical, improvisational, dynamic world of the Italian street theatre with the neoclassical, seventeenth-century French elegance and brilliance of verbal wit so typical of Molière's comedies.

The greatest of all writers of French comedy employed most of comedy's traditional forms. As an actor and a leader of an acting troupe, Molière was familiar with every form of stage performance in Paris and the provinces, including the works of other famous playwrights, old-fashioned farces, and the popular commedia dell'arte troupes. Molière found an inspiration for his dramatic efforts in the tradition of literary comedy, yet his works represent a fascinating blend of styles that defies simple classification. Molière's comedies require a sound understanding of the principles of comic writing and the nature and function of humor. Additionally, they challenge actors to demonstrate and incorporate a wide variety of comic acting techniques into performance.

As Andrew Calder put it, "Molière combines subject, characters, dia-

lectic, and plot in such a way that all work together to provide a co-
herent action which unfolds with regularity and a strong sense of in-
evitability from the beginning of the first act to the end of the fifth."[2]
The comedies are classic examples of combinations of various comic
writing devices. They often include series of plot complications, dramatic irony, discrepant awareness and ignorance of characters, incongru-
ous actions and juxtaposition of oppositions, surprises and unexpected
turns of events, trust and deception, reversal and contradiction, tension built through repetition, chance and coincidences, a considerable
amount of physical action, and a comic denouement that brings balance
and harmony.

Comedy is anchored in incongruity and surprise, imbalance and absurdity, aggressiveness and cruelty, or repetition and extremes, and the actor's choices need to reflect a corresponding interest in the extraordinary.
Elements of comedy manifest themselves in all of Molière's plays—and
respectively in every character and every scene of *The School for Wives*—
through the relationships and interactions between characters, their in-
congruous actions and surprising behavior, or juxtaposition of the reality of the play and the reality of the audience.

As an acting pedagogue, coach, and director, I have discovered that
the complexity of Molière's works often overwhelms actors, and they
therefore do not know where to start the exploration. I devised a series of activities that allow actors to focus on a single aspect of performing and place an emphasis on each one of the aforementioned con-
siderations. Through exploration, actors discover an effortless way to
synthesize physical and vocal choices, emotional depth, and intellectual
ideas. Act 2, scene 2 of *The School for Wives* provides a clear example of
contrasting characters, clear relationships and objectives, quick pace and
verbal exchanges, specific physical action, and a blend of high and low
comedy.

The plot of *The School for Wives* revolves around Arnolphe, a forty-
two-year-old, powerful, possessive, selfish, and confident owner of the
house, who is painfully afraid of the possibility of being cuckolded by
an educated wife. Therefore, he has kept Agnes, a young, naive, and
simple girl, ignorant for thirteen years so that he can safely marry her
without the danger of deceit. According to his plan, not knowing about
the complexity of the world, she will trust his lessons, follow his lead,
and fulfill his every wish. Unfortunately for Arnolphe, Agnes's lack of
experience, which he initially nurtures and cherishes, becomes the Tro-
jan horse for Horace, a young and attractive suitor who steals her heart
during Arnolphe's absence. During the course of the play, Arnolphe per-
sistently creates new plans to prevent Agnes from meeting her new ac-

quaintance, but fate always favors the lovers. Through the magical power of love, Agnes discovers ways to outsmart Arnolphe and unmask his true intentions.

Act 2, scene 2 finds Arnolphe questioning and scolding his servants for letting a man into his house despite strict instructions against it. He has just discovered that the youngster who came had a chance to be alone with Agnes and had fallen in love with her. Horace has just left the scene after sharing with Arnolphe his excitement of his new relationship with the naive and innocent girl. Understandably, Arnolphe is furious and summons the servants.

The following suggested acting approaches may be done simultaneously by four different groups of actors working on the same scene. Another option is for one group of actors to explore each one of the approaches one after the other. After about ten to fifteen minutes of exploration with a particular approach, the scenes should be performed in front of other actors who should participate in a brief discussion on the observed methods, comparing and contrasting the different techniques.

The first approach focuses solely on the vocal exploration with an emphasis on language, verse, phrasing, and vocal choices for the characters. The actors should limit the physical aspects of the presentation to a minimum and focus their attention on all aspects of verbal communication and characterization. Multiple vocal techniques, related to scansion and verse, pace, tempo, phrasing, emphasis, vocal variety, and expressiveness, as well as language devices, should be explored to discover the wide variety of choices available to actors.

The journey will need to begin with attention to scansion, verse, and the Alexandrine verse (translated into iambic pentameter). Wilbur's translations always give apparent visual clues to actors working on tempo in vocal delivery and phrasing. Often the verse is intact yet includes a number of exchanges between all three characters within a single line:

ARNOLPHE. Well, speak! Come, hurry. Quickly! Time is fleeting!
Let's hear it! Speak!
ALAIN AND GEORGETTE.
      Oh! Oh!
GEORGETTE.
       My heart's stopped beating.
ALAIN. I'm dying.
ARNOLPHE.   I'm sweating, and I need some air.
I must calm down; I'll walk around the square.

To maintain the pulse and rhythm of the verse, the dialogue requires a certain pace to keep rhyme apparent and verse intact. Quick pace reveals the conflict in the scene and builds tension. Consequently, "topping" becomes an extremely important and effective technique. "Pace is achieved by doing away with all meaningless pauses,"[3] so actors need to experiment with avoiding pointless pauses and picking up cues without delay. With the fast tempo of verbal exchange and growing tension, it becomes necessary to pay strict attention to clarity of speech and articulation.

In addition to pace and tempo, actors may explore humor in delivering funny lines through interesting and imaginative phrasing, rapid shift in rhythm, special emphasis on single words or phrases, and variations in tone. Janet Suzman observes that "comic acting relies largely on what an actor can do with a specific word to make it funny."[4] Key words may be emphasized by force, pause before or after, prolongation of the word, or deliberate inflection.[5] The tempo can shift from topping each other's tone and almost overlapping lines to slowing down while drastically changing the tone (undercutting). The rhythm can be altered by rapid delivery followed by sudden stops and vice versa.

A comic effect can be created by experimenting with the tone and quality of the voice of each character or by selection of a specific speech pattern for the character. Naturally, comedy explores unusual sounds, speech irregularities, speech impairments, stutter, mumbling, odd and atypical speech patterns, variety in pitch and tone, and other devices. Any of these may be applied to Molière's text as well. Certainly, the weirdness should not be self-contained but rather based on the peculiarity of the character's self, but changes in the emotional state of Arnolphe, for example, may be supported by fluctuation in vocal characteristics, so that one is suddenly replaced by its exact opposite: fast speech suddenly slowed down, sudden silence replaces eloquence, low energy follows a hyper energy, or any other unexpected change in voice usage that actors may wish to explore.

In the scene above, Arnolphe is far more eloquent than the servants Alain and Georgette, yet humorous effect may be achieved through creating a contrast between the vocal choices for the characters (Arnolphe vs. Alain and Georgette) or contrasting choices for the servants themselves. Experimenting with finding nonverbal manifestations of the servants' feelings and attitudes while Arnolphe verbally expresses himself often brings humor forward.

Successful comic actors are certain about the meaning of a text and are able to grasp humor and convey it to the audience. Although in most cases humor is set in the text itself, comedy often becomes fertile ground for an actor's exploration of subtext as a source for humorous effect. Some of the most interesting actors demonstrate a variety of possibilities for conveying meaning through text and subtext.

Molière's comedies rely to a large extent on verbal humor; therefore, the audience will want to be able to hear every word of the play. No matter what choice for a character's vocal quality or speech pattern an actor makes, it will not be appreciated if meaning, and thus humor, is lost. Whether the actors exploring the scene utilize a unique voice usage, monotones or fluctuation, very slow or very fast tempo, correct or incorrect emphasis on words, unusual pause or strange rhythm of speech, all choices need to be characterized by clear, well-articulated speech, with particular attention to the last word of the sentence. Sometimes a key word in a line is the final one and if lost, the meaning of the whole sentence is lost, too.

The second approach focuses specifically on the physical expression of the characters' intentions and relationships, physical confrontation, and interaction between characters. It requires that the staging emphasize and highlight farcical elements of the scene, frantic energy, fast pace, a range of tempo and rhythm of movement, and full stage usage.

Although Molière's comedies lack stage directions and description of physical actions, the influences of commedia dell'arte and the French farces are recognizable, especially in scenes that involve physical interaction between masters and servants. Alain and Georgette, Arnolphe's servants in *The School for Wives*, are the most consistent and unchangeable characters in the play who are easily associated with the original stock characters of commedia dell'arte. They offer possibilities for actors to focus on physical aspects of characterization and demonstrate acrobatic skills and alteration of physical characteristics typical for the *zanni* in the Italian commedia. The humorous effect is further reinforced by juxtaposition of Arnolphe's and Alain's and Georgette's physical choices. Of course, the two servants should explore some contrast between the two of them in energy level, pace, tempo, rhythm, flexibility, and agility and should relate them to the different kinds of servants in commedia.

The variety of physical choices for the characters may be explored throughout the scene to heighten the humor of the situation, including alteration of physical characteristics, elastic face and body, exaggeration, understatement, or distortion of body posture or movement based on a character trait. Actors may jump, twist themselves into shapes, do "funny walking," or anything their creative mind may suggest.[6] In the spirit of the masked commedia, actors can use faces or parts of their faces, such as eyes, eyebrows, cheeks, or lips, to reveal feelings and attitudes, to respond to lines or actions of other characters, or to silently communicate the subtext or their reactions to the audience through exaggerated lively expression or complete lack of emotion.

The physical aspect of Molière's comedies may be further explored through shifts in tempo, rhythm, energy, and careful selection of comic gestures and "business," which appear to be most efficient when used to illuminate the action or the characters. Some actors are tempted to be funny in some extraneous way, using tricks that are not related to the moment; but, as Seyler puts it, it is bad taste "pursuing a laugh which is irrelevant to the scene in hand."[7]

In *The School for Wives* all of the scenes in which Alain and Georgette interact with Arnolphe involve some kind of violent physical activity that aims to punish the servants or teach them a lesson. Arnolphe's lines in act 2, scene 2 also suggest a possibility for physical interaction between him and Georgette and Alain, and it seems apparent that from the moment he enters the scene, Arnolphe is repeatedly trying to stop his servants from running away from him:

> Hush! Both of you come here:
> This way, this way. Come, hurry! Do as you're told!

Several lines later:

> You cursèd scoundrels, while I was gone you let
> A man into this house—No, not just yet!
> Tell me at once—Don't move!—I want you two
> To tell me—Whff! I mean to learn from you—
> If anyone moves, I'll squash him like a louse.
> Now tell me, how did that man get into my house?
> Well, speak! Come, hurry. Quickly! Time is fleeting!

And finally:

> I'm sweating, and I need some air.
> I must calm down: I'll walk around the square.

The whole scene should be explored as a chase scene that involves broad physical humor and slapstick. Frequently used in comedy, and particularly in farce, are physical accidents, such as slapping or bumping into each other, which usually involve bodily injuries. Often humor lies in an intense physical activity including precise synchronized movement, as well as comic fights, runs, rolls, hits, or falls. Often tension builds to a point in which one of the most popular forms of physical action, a chase scene, develops. The actors who are playing Alain and Georgette should have as a goal to avoid at any cost the direct physical contact with their master; while the goal of Arnolphe would be to get them to come close so that, in his rage, he can physically punish them for their negligence and disobedience. During their onstage "chase," all three actors should try to engage in a variety of physical encounters.

Our humor has become more verbal and less physical,[8] and this is the reason that inexperienced actors turn more often to means of vocal expression rather than physical exploration of a role. Yet movement or stillness, chosen wisely, used selectively, and executed with precision and control, often substitutes for words. Body language is an extremely powerful tool, particularly when contrasted to language or situation. Incongruity between what has been said and what a body reveals to be the truth of the situation or character undermines the power of words and intensifies humor.

The third approach focuses on an actor's realistic representation of the role. Within the framework of the play, an emphasis must be placed on believability, sincerity, genuine belief in the character's point of view, serious attitude, specificity, and truth.

Comedy does not depict reality as it is, and it searches for stylized signs and expressions. Hence, actors in Molière's comedies are not tied in small, realistic activities but rather explore symbols to communicate ideas. Everything about his characters becomes heightened, including their personalities, peculiarities, ideas, and lifestyles, and in turn, it permits a freedom of choice in their physical appearance, vocal life, and behavior. Nevertheless, beneath those enlargements from the norm and despite the added emphasis on technique, successful performance of Molière's characters requires that actors employ absolute truthfulness to character.

In Molière's comedy all dramatis personae's actions and choices are prompted by their ideas of truth, and because they are usually being overdrawn or are out of relation to the cause, they become funny. Molière's characters have a single weakness or shortcoming that is blown out of proportion. The defect is an overriding passion that overrules the life and the fate of a character. Comic exaggerations and characters' extreme behavior and actions are amusing because they are based on the truth about the character and on her or his genuine belief in her or his distorted perspective.

Seyler observes, "Comedy seems to be the standing outside a character or situation and pointing out one's delight in certain aspects of it."[9] Great actors understand and trust the comedic quality of a part and play and establish direct contact with the audience. As a result, a special, delicate, psychological bond between the two sides appears. Acting in Molière's comedies entails fluctuating between a full awareness of the audience and the actor's ability to disregard it when necessary. Exploring the truth about the character brings an awareness of the comic point of view, including the character's perspective and the juxtaposition to the actor/audience's perspective.[10]

Therefore, exploration of truth will include an actor's basic character analysis for realistic theatre,[11] including given circumstances, Stanislavski's "magic if," super objectives, obstacles, specific character relationships, detailed choices and ideas for the characters, strategies and tactics, text and subtext.[12] The exercise requires stripping down the characters to their simple, absolute core as believable, real, sincere, objective-driven individuals with past, present, and future. Actors should focus on listening and responding to each other, on open communication and expression of ideas, and on sharing their emotional state with the audience.

For example, the actors performing Alain and Georgette, instead of focusing on the commedia's influence or the characteristics of the Italian stock characters, should attempt to create realistic portrayals of two friends who happen to be servants in Arnolphe's house. They know they have done something wrong, and, feeling regretful, they want to devise a plan together to avoid punishment. Throughout the scene Arnolphe questions them and tries to make them feel guilty for disobeying him; the servants try to make him forgive them through various tactics, including flirting, fainting, trying to make him laugh, or angering him so that he will let them go. The emotions of the characters are profound and sincere: the servants feel remorse, and Arnolphe is completely and genuinely devastated by the possibility of losing the love of his life, Agnes, forever. Through his asides he shares his real feelings and pain, searching for understanding and empathy: "I'll mute my rage as well as I know how; / Patience, my wounded heart! Beat softly, now!" (2.2).

Despite the fact that performance in classical comedy is grounded in exaggeration, lack of balance, and distortion, the need exists to create believable characters beneath the comic mask. This does not necessarily mean that actors create realistic portrayals but rather complex individuals. No matter how extreme, Molière's characters should be connected to the reality of the play, and as Richardson argues, "Comedy characters must feel and think just like the rest of us; in fact their emotions are bigger and so are their attempts to achieve their goals."[13] Yet since comedy presents a distorted mirror of reality, actors' choices include a special "one step beyond reality," which allows them to exploit exaggeration and intensification while keeping immediacy and honesty of the character.

The final approach emphasizes a variety of comic acting techniques and elements of comedy. Physical and vocal choices should be explored to emphasize the extreme contrast between the characters in a scene, reflect unexpected changes in attitude, energy, or emotional state, or bring incongruity and surprise.

Extremes generate laughter. Molière has already given Arnolphe a maniacal fear of cuckoldry. Arnolphe's exaggerated passion is joined by exaggerated self-assertiveness. His feelings are also tremendous: he moves easily from outrage to calmness, from overexcitement to lack of expression, and from reason to obsession. Everything in Molière's characters may be exaggerated: behavior, actions, words, or manners. Exaggeration of physical characteristics, vocal choices, or personality traits as a common source of comic invention is especially effective if presented in opposing pairs, such as setting foolish naiveté against sophisticated intellectualism or juxtaposing servants' frankness, simplicity, and lack of class to their master's skill for intrigues, refined games, and elegance.

Repetition of contrast between expectations and consequence, anticipated by the characters or by the audience, creates a snowballing humorous effect. Most jokes result from setting up an expectation that is then unfulfilled, or the associations in the listener's mind depart from it. For example, Arnolphe's absolute confidence in the rightness of his actions and illusion that everything will go according to his plan and the proof in reality of his mistakes brings about humor that is reinforced by the audience's knowledge of things unknown to or unexpected by his character.

Comedy depends on careful listening and a timely reply to other characters in the scene. Seyler compares this timing to a rally at tennis—the quicker one returns the impact of a remark, the sooner the audience will enjoy the hit. Actors should do everything possible to prevent letting the ball drop. Instead, they should try to "catch the spectator's breath with a smashing return."[14] A comic effect is produced by an unexpected reaction rather than by what has been said; or, as Richardson explains, "The joke is not the man throwing the pie, the joke is the face it lands on."[15]

Another favored comic technique that may be used is the take, or a physical way of showing surprise, an explosive show of shock that occurs midway. The take is based on the nonimmediate realization that "adds to the observer's anticipation and increases the degree of surprise."[16] The double take is even funnier. It is a delayed recognition and unfolds in four distinct movements: a character takes a look at something very surprising, but there is no immediate reaction; the character returns to her or his previous normal focus; suddenly the character is hit by the realization with a double-quick return to take another look, followed by a big reaction of surprise. A double take may be made into a triple take, if the suddenness of realization is split.

Contrary to the quickness of the take, the slow burn extends the beginning of the realization and shares it with the audience, and it is a reaction to some kind of put-down. The deadpan is even subtler than the slow burn. It is the most extreme form of "playing against," a technique that gives a great focus to an action by letting the audience do all the filling in and consciously refusing to reveal the character's reaction.[17]

Comic gestures and "business" and the rule of the three may be explored with a repetition of action or business used to create a snowball effect. Suddenly, on the third time, a new action is introduced, or the previous one is executed with slight alteration. Plot, language, and character development devices may be explored to discover and heighten humor in the scene.

The nature of comedy encompasses a unique fusion of intensity and effortlessness, and it requires the same blend of opposites from actors performing in it. They need to direct the audience's attention toward one perspective and then successfully surprise the audience with another, but in order to do so, they make sure that the audience's focus does not wander and that their own actions are controlled and coordinated with their partners' actions.[18]

The four selected approaches provoke the most immediate response in actors. Compared back to back, each one of them creates a different yet interesting and thought-provoking humorous scene. The verbal approach tends to bring attention to the meaning of the words, creating a sophisticated, intellectual feel for the play. The physical approach brings attention to the action, revealing dynamics in the scene and allowing the contrast between the social ranks of the characters to shine. The realistic approach reveals emotional levels and complexity of the character, exploring believability and contributing to the contemporary feel to the play. The comic techniques approach illuminates the many possibilities for discovering humor in any moment of the play.

Certainly, no choice of approach should be used with the sole purpose of provoking laughter. For example, too much physical action between lines or within a line, as well as use of multiple takes, comic business, and pauses, may upset the rhythm of a scene and fail to communicate meaning. Richard Wilbur, in the preface to his *Tartuffe* translation, advises actors and directors to be careful with purposeful insertion of too much physical action or overemphasizing of farcical elements. He believes that even a simple reading of Molière's text itself may provide a complete experience of the work: "Trust the words to convey the point and persons of the comedy, and trust them also to be sufficiently entertaining."[19] Similarly, extensive focus on the verbal aspect may break the rhythm of the action and slow down the tempo, causing the play to become boring and uninteresting. Too strong a focus on realism, however, would distance the audience from the exaggerated style of classical comedy, thus dragging the play down and losing the humor.

One of the hardest things for actors of all ages appears to be achieving unity of voice, body, and mind of the character. The major conclusion that actors come to after experimentation with the four approaches is that no single one of them is sufficient to master the acting in Molière's plays. Approaches are not mutually exclusive; rather they layer different nuances of the performance. Naturally, actors combine all four aspects when they work on each approach. For example, they cannot completely disregard movement when working on voice, or they cannot block their vocal choices while working on a chase scene, thus proving once more that voice, body, and mind influence each other and are interrelated.

Certainly, the four methods are not the only ones that may be helpful in mastering the acting in Molière's comedies. There are at least two more that are of equal importance to the actor but have not been selected for detailed review here because of the impossibility to achieve complete effect on the actor within ten to fifteen minutes of exploration. One of the approaches is related to the manners, morals, rules, and social masks of seventeenth-century France. Molière character portrayals will be complete only after the actor gains an extensive knowledge and understanding of public and private conduct, rules of acceptance and disapproval, and ways to succeed in the time of Molière. Understandably, the actor needs to utilize to the fullest external elements such as costumes, props, sets, and space in order to create the comic mask of the character. Although external elements are often chosen and defined by directors and designers, some of the world's most famous unforgettable comic characters have been created by actors who have discovered a unique way to wear their costumes or handle their props.

The other approach is more theoretical and requires understanding of the satirical genius of Molière. Comedy has always found ways to ridicule people, ideas, institutions, or circumstances, thus making spectators feel superior. It focuses on foolish or asocial actions of humankind, on ideas and political institutions that are believed to be wrong, or on any characteristic that appears—to the majority in that place and at that time— abnormal and needs punishment or correction. With Molière's works, character portrayal in the comedy of intrigue reached its highest development. Because Molière focused on character, the plot was subordinated and simple. Characters represented all levels of society.[20] Often the abnormality of the central character was sharply outlined against a background of social normality, and morality was based on an enlightened common sense.[21] Theorists maintain that the audience laughs observing weaknesses and flaws of others and comparing them with the greatness in oneself, or as Helitzer asserts, "[H]umor is oriented to maintaining the status quo by ridiculing deviant social behavior and reassures the majority member that his way of life is proper and free from ridicule."[22]

Molière's comedies offer endless possibilities for creativity and imagination. Naturally, comic elements in the play and the full comic potential of character will be discovered through rehearsal, yet exploration of the four approaches will confirm that many right directions in working with Molière exist and that a synthesized approach needs to be developed for performing Molière's or any other classical comedies.

Notes

1. Richard Wilbur, trans., *Molière: "The School for Wives" and "The Learned Ladies"* (San Diego: Harcourt Brace, 1997). Wilbur's translation of Molière's play has been used throughout this essay.

2. Andrew Calder, *Molière: The Theory and Practice of Comedy* (New York: Athlone Press, 1993), 34.

3. Don Richardson, *Acting without Agony: An Alternative to the Method* (Boston: Allyn and Bacon, 1988), 128.

4. Janet Suzman, *Acting with Shakespeare: The Comedies* (New York: Applause, 1996), 76.

5. Stanley Kahan and Kenneth W. Rugg, *Introduction to Acting* (Boston: Allyn and Bacon, 1998), 116.

6. Arthur Asa Berger, *The Art of Comedy Writing* (New York: Transaction, 1992), 47.

7. Athene Seyler and Stephen Haggard, *The Craft of Comedy* (London: Routledge, 1981), 48.

8. Melvin Helitzer, *Comedy Techniques for Writers & Performers: The HEARTS Theory of Humor Writing* (Athens, OH: Lawhead, 1984), 48.

9. Seyler and Haggard, *The Craft of Comedy*, 9–10.

10. Paul Kuritz, *Fundamental Acting: A Practical Guide* (New York: Applause, 1998), 123.

11. See Constantin Stanislavski, *An Actor Prepares; Building a Character; Creating a Role,* trans. Elizabeth Reynolds Hapgood (New York: Routledge, 1989).

12. See Robert Barton, *Acting Onstage and Off* (Belmont, CA: Thomson, Wadsworth, 2005).

13. Richardson, *Acting without Agony,* 118.

14. Seyler and Haggard, *The Craft of Comedy,* 46–47.

15. Richardson, *Acting without Agony,* 129.

16. John Harrop and Sabin R. Epstein, *Acting with Style* (Englewood Cliffs, NJ: Prentice-Hall, 1982), 175.

17. Ibid.

18. Kuritz, *Fundamental Acting*, 123.

19. Wilbur, introduction to *Molière: "The School for Wives,"* vi.

20. Jerry L. Crawford and Joan Snyder, *Acting in Person and in Style* (Las Vegas: University of Nevada Press, 1976), 180.

21. Willard Smith, *The Nature of Comedy* (Boston: Richard G. Badger, 1930), 123–26.

22. Helitzer, *Comedy Techniques for Writers & Performers,* 31–32.

The Laugh Factory?

Humor and Horror at
Le Théâtre du Grand Guignol

Felicia J. Ruff

JEAN ARAGNY and Francis Neilson's *Le baiser de sang* opens with the following stage direction and dialogue:

[Professor Leduc and Dr. Volguine are wearing surgical masks as the curtain rises. Stage right, dressed head to foot in white, the Male Nurse stands next to the trolley. . . . The Patient is a bald man. He is in pain, in spite of the chloroform, stirring and crying out from time to time.

A cross-shaped incision has been made on the forehead above the right eye. The flaps of skin are clipped back so that the frontal bone of the skull. is exposed. Holes have been drilled in the trepanning drill. Everybody is leaning over, with outstretched necks, and attentively following the Professor's every move.]

PROF. LEDUC. It's no good. It's not going to work. The lesion means that I'm going to have to drill here . . . and not here after all . . . there's no alternative.
DR. VOLGUINE. That's the most resistant spot.
LEDUC. Yes. A compress . . . and another . . . and another one . . . a swab . . . how's his pulse?
VOLGUINE. Very weak.
LEDUC. What about his legs? Are they cold?
VOLGUINE. Very cold.
LEDUC. (raising his eyelids, then raising his eyes upwards): I only hope he's not going to give us any trouble with his circulation like the Dutchman the other day. Get the caffeine ready, a small amount. (The Male Nurse bustles about.) Swab! (He begins to drill. The Patient stirs.) Just a moment! (The Professor stops drilling. Volguine hands him a stethoscope. He listens.) This is bad . . . give him a jab immediately. (He listens) This is bad.

(Volguine gives an injection.) Let's do this quickly. (He succeeds in drilling the hole. The Patient groans almost silently. The Professor hands back the stethoscope.) All done.
VOLGUINE. I can't feel a pulse.

Within seconds they pronounce the patient dead, lamenting that "he was brought in . . . ten minutes too late."[1]

A man has just died, a scenario that seems poorly designed to prompt laughter. Truth be told, however, I laughed really hard when I saw the play performed this fall by a New York company, Blood Brothers, and not because it was poorly done. Quite the contrary. When I found myself laughing, which I did several times during the scenes of graphic violence, I immediately had these reflexive moments, "What does this say about me?" and "What must my friend think of me?" Originally, the play debuted in 1929 as part of Le Théâtre du Grand Guignol's season. This notorious French theatre remains famous for having staged plays of horror that featured scenes of graphic violence. Today the term *Grand Guignol* has evolved into an adjective, accurately conjuring images of blood and gore. But this company of artists, who entertained through scenes of strangling, limb-severing, disemboweling, and maiming, among numerous other tortures, deliberately incorporated laughter into the macabre entertainment.

Grand Guignol is perhaps an appropriately bizarre topic in an academic consideration of comedy; however, Grand Guignol merits serious study because this horror theatre employed comedy and laughter very strategically. Like a variety show, a night at the Grand Guignol featured at least three or four short plays; from Grand Guignol's inception, a night's performance featured scenes of horror alternating with one-act comedies. The integration of comedy was designed to offer more than simple comic relief. Grand Guignol is a theatre of extremes, most especially extreme emotional states, and by comingling fear and laughter, the theatre artists manipulate the audience. A term was designated that summarized the emotional roller coaster an audience member experienced: *douche ecossaise,* a hot and cold shower.[2] An examination of the function of comedy at Le Théâtre du Grand Guignol from historical, performative, and generic perspectives raises the specter of the relationship between humor and horror. Since this performance tradition consciously strove to provoke laughter, important questions are raised regarding comedy and genre categories. A night at the Grand Guignol negotiates laughter and terror, bringing into focus a point that theorists have been grappling with for millennia, the question of why we laugh at another's suffering.[3]

As a producing organization, Le Théâtre du Grand Guignol first thrived then survived, beginning in 1897 and ultimately closing in 1962. Before the name came to mean horror theatre, *Grand Guignol* originally referred to a theatre building, a converted church located on the rue Chaptal in Paris in Montmartre. Oscar Méténier, journalist and private secretary to the police commissioner of Paris, founded Le Théâtre du Grand Guignol as an extension of the naturalist aesthetic principles of the Théâtre Libre. Like his mentor André Antoine, Méténier strove to accurately reproduce life on the stage. But his subject matter turned to true-life sordid crime stories, his *comédies rosses*. Méténier's two-year term was followed by Max Maurey, who formulated many of the Grand Guignol's more recognizable features, in part through his assemblage of a company of playwrights, technicians, and actors. He contracted numerous playwrights, including René Berton, Maurice Level, and, the "Prince of Terror" himself, André de Lorde, among many others. He employed a stage manager, Paul Ratineau, who acted for the company and took on the responsibility for much of the mise-en-scène, designing lights, sound, makeup, and the all-important props. Maurey's production methods were further consolidated under Camille Choisy, who ran the theatre from 1915 to 1927. Several other producers followed, but it was the early period where the theatre's most characteristic artistic practices were formulated. Producers were important not only to the Grand Guignol's financial survival but also to establishing successful artistic policies. A group of actors completed the company; these included the celebrated Paula Maxa, who reputedly died more than ten thousand times through sixty different means, and L. Paulais, known as the Mounet-Sully of the Grand Guignol.

Theatrical staging strategies were intimately intertwined with dramaturgy at Le Théâtre du Grand Guignol, all of which were designed to provoke very specific audience reactions. Richard J. Hand and Michael Wilson, two major scholars of the genre, say, "A performance at the Grand-Guignol in the Maurey/Choisy-mould strove to terrify and titillate the spectator through a mixture of horror, laughter and the erotic. A typical evening's entertainment reveals a sophisticated exploitation of the contemporary audience's fears, taboos and desire."[4] The audience is an important component of Grand Guignol aesthetics. Perhaps motivated more by marketing than medical need, a house doctor was allegedly placed on the payroll to attend to the fainting spectators. And perhaps a doctor was required as onstage action confronted the audience with a range of gruesome visuals, from eye gouging to beheading. No matter how revolting the act, stage artifice required verisimilitude. Therefore, precise, predetermined blocking was designed to integrate the actor's physical actions with the scenery and props. The aesthetic demands on the actors and technicians in Grand Guignol, as in much comedy such as slapstick, had to be carefully synchronized and preset. The small stage was populated with props utilized by actors in tour-de-force performances of manically paced action. This put certain demands on the actor. In his excellent study on Grand Guignol aesthetics, František Deák emphasizes that actors were required "to render the exact outward signs of feeling and at the same time execute the tricks with precision and coordination."[5] Like actors in farces, Grand Guignol performers found themselves simultaneously embodying a character, while dexterously wielding all sorts of props, such as scalpels, knives, and needles, with the skill of a magician.

Grand Guignol plays demand recognizable settings to add to the believability of the circumstances, which leads to the issue of locale. These horror plays, like much farce, locate their situations in bedrooms, hospital rooms, prisons, and mental institutions. Thus location aligns compellingly with subject matter: adultery, sexual revenge, criminality, illness, insanity—topics that address the violation of bourgeois moral values. While this French form is radical in its choice of subject matter and its amoral universe, it is not particularly innovative in its dramaturgic strategies. The Well-Made-Play structure girds the plays, although the form is defied by the lack of normative social values, particularly at the play's end. The short Grand Guignol plays are not where virtue gets rewarded and vice punished. Despite being very structurally measured, the short play form does provide an alternative that contrasts with the more developed narrative of a full-length play. Daniel Gerould, in his book *Gallant and Libertine,* which looks at short dramatic forms of eighteenth-century France, gives a good summary of what fuels the short play: "They violate traditional expectations of established dramatic modes; they subvert the demands of ruling dogmas; they offer escape from reigning conventions and canons. Short forms start and stop abruptly. They avoid the architectonically predictable in favor of spontaneity and surprise."[6] This is certainly true of the Grand Guignol aesthetic strategy and one place where humor and horror meet as both, in this context, are designed to assault bourgeois pieties. But, while each of these short plays is individual and complete in itself, they are parts of a whole experience.

And this places another demand on Grand Guignol actors, who had to be able to perform in each genre in one evening. After a scene of horror, as Hand and Wilson say, "the actor would shortly be on stage again, this time endeavoring to master the rapid-fire innuendo and physical romps of Grand-Guignol comedy."[7] In both plays of horror and comedy physical adroitness and keen timing were of prime importance to the actor. One distinguishing characteristic for the actor in each genre was pace; while horror plays generally begin slowly then strategically pick up speed, deliberately utilizing silence, the evening's farces run at a quick pace. Nevertheless, a sense of timing is essential in both types of performance.

The extreme subject matter lends itself to an exaggerated acting style, evidencing an almost cartoonish element in Grand Guignol performance. On some level Grand Guignol finds its aesthetic roots in nineteenth-century *fait divers,* which were printed news accounts that sensationalized grisly crime stories through bold illustrations. As the theatre scholar Mel Gordon says, these "prefigured exactly on the printed page what the Grand Guignol would be on stage."[8] Similarly sensationalistic are the advertising posters. The design element of Grand Guignol often emphasizes caricature, highlighting the exaggerated expression that is reflected in the strange grimaces and the heightened gestures that lead to near-camp performances. The cartoonish exaggeration in no way implies, however, that audiences were to laugh at a performance. Laughter is more a spontaneous, physical reaction in the audience, while the heightened onstage physicality evidences the extreme subject matter. After all, how can an actor be subtle as he cuts off his own hand or gouges out a young woman's eyes?

While laughter can be appropriate at the Grand Guignol, directors and actors had to delicately negotiate their theatricality to avoid provoking misdirected laughter. Actors were aware of their limits. As Maxa, the Grand Guignol star, said:

> From my first performance, I had to learn my trade harshly. Often one word, one sentence said a little too fast, a little too brutally caused a laugh. . . . The atmosphere was tense, nerves on edge, a mere nothing could cause laughter. In the case of a mistake, I was completely abashed. When the atmosphere was lost, it was necessary to regain it, which was sometimes very hard and often impossible."[9]

Thus every performance detail had to be carefully executed. Like a Feydeau farce (and Maxa performed in Feydeau farces as well as the Grand Guignol) every word, every prop, every action in a Grand Guignol play has its importance, thus engaging the audience in a careful watching and reading of the performance. It is not surprising that the author, actor, and director collaborated very closely. In terms of genre categories, Grand Guignol performance may most closely align with farce. Not coincidentally, Feydeau farces ruled the Boulevard in Paris as Grand Guignol aesthetic practices took shape. Farce and Grand Guignol meet on various levels. Both carefully construct the audience experience; both rely on staging ordinary, flesh-and-blood people who speak recognizable dialogue and live in familiar places; both blend a precisely constructed performance with outrageous madness. Furthermore, both farce and Grand Guignol praxis position the playwright and director as godlike puppeteers who let their characters loose in an aberrant universe. Fittingly, Méténier chose the term *Grand Guignol* as a reference to "Big Puppets" or "Puppets for Big People."

Well-known authors such as Sacha Guitry, Octave Mirbeau, and Henri Duvernois contributed comedies to Grand Guignol theatre. Two notable writers in the company's stable, who wrote both comedies and plays of horror, were Andre de Lorde and René Berton. A medical doctor, Berton wrote numerous plays on medical subjects or themes. His comedy *Après Coup! . . . ou Tics* serves as a fine example of a comedy written for performance amid plays of horror. The play features standard motifs of Grand Guignol (whether horror or comedy): the medical profession and the question of physical infirmity. However, nothing physically violent or revolting is put on display in this twenty-minute performance. The location is a bourgeois home; however, since the owner, Dr. Martin, is a physician, this means that any room of the house can suddenly become a private examination chamber. The two dinner guests soon take advantage of their host by soliciting free medical advice. His male counterpart, M. de Merliot, confesses to a peculiar physiological quirk, or tic: immediately after orgasm, Merliot admits, he is incapable of speaking. This has an upside with his wife—he can simply turn over and go to sleep—but frustrates his mistresses, who desire to engage in pillow talk. Later the doctor confesses to suffering from his own postcoital tic: a leg spasm.

Infidelity and jealousy are standard Grand Guignol subjects and are dealt with candidly here. Madame Martin, threatened by the physical attributes of her female guest, challenges her husband and establishes the play's comic premise when she tells him: "Remember what I said— an eye for an eye!" (A rather gruesome reference given the larger performance context.) Dr. Martin, the husband, accurately translates this as "a hump for a hump!"[10] Berton's play is filled with double entendres, particularly regarding sex, such as references to "enjoying a good ride," which references the couple's arrival by automobile; remembering that the play premiered in 1908 underscores how Grand Guignol, like melodrama, thrives on contemporary inventions—electricity, telephones, automobiles.

Doctors function centrally in many Grand Guignol plays. Voyeurism is fundamental here as it is, I suspect, to all comedy. Doctors are often in the position to examine their patients, directing the audiences' gaze over the body of the complainant; the spectator and doctor evaluate the infirmity together. Furthermore, there is the expectation of trust in the touch and gaze of a doctor ("First do no harm"); therefore, when, whether in farce or horror fiction, a doctor looks or touches inappropriately, there is something not only dishonorable but creepy in the violation. Unethical doctors appear in many farces as they use their professional position to cop a feel; Joe Orton's Dr. Prentice, from the 1969 *What the Butler Saw*, immediately gets Miss Geraldine Barclay of the Friendly Faces Employment Bureau to undress as a part of her job interview. In Berton's sex farce his main character, Dr. Martin, rejects the stethoscope in favor of placing his head on his patient's substantial cleavage. While no assignations are seen onstage, the men are seen immediately afterward, first exhibiting Martin as his leg twitches and spasms. When asked, "Was it good for you?" Dr. Martin responds, "How can you ask? It was literally so good I'm literally wild with—(He stands and his leg shakes madly)."[11] These physical antics could be perfectly realized by a comedian with the physical skills of, say, Dick Van Dyke. Before long, the other couple's infidelity is in evidence as Madame Martin returns with a stammering Monsieur de Merliot. Both men end up together, struggling to hide their respective tics, eventually being waited on by a butler—who is barking like a dog, evidence of his own sexual encounter with a serving girl. The play ends with the three men respectively barking, stammering, and twitching.

The notion of physical infirmity prompting laughter is common in fin-de-siècle French performance. Numerous scholars have linked certain turn-of-the-century performance styles with contemporary physiological response theory, examining the nineteenth-century fascination with tics, grimaces, and convulsive movements in connection with artistic interpretation as evidenced in song-stylings, clowning, cabaret performances, and early film. One example is French literary scholar Beth Rae Gordon, who finds links among entertainers' physical and vocal styles with academic study of epilepsy, the all-inclusive "hysteria," and mesmerism. Gordon focuses on "a previously unnoticed relation between a significant cultural and aesthetic style and the extraordinary upsurge of concern with and diagnosis of hysteria and epilepsy in late nineteenth-century French medical practice and theory. Parallel studies of suggestion and unconscious imitation, similarly, have considerable pertinence for spectatorship in the same period."[12] Grand Guignol performance is clearly an extension of this nineteenth-century tradition, intermingling as it does the performer and spectator's physiological response. *Tics* author, Dr. René Berton, is clearly indicating contemporary neurological response theories in his farce, while exploiting the fashion for poking fun at physical infirmity.

Still, all in all the fun in this brief farcical interlude was an alternative to the physical tortures partnered with comedy. Comedy and horror meet at Le Théâtre du Grand Guignol as both exploit a fear of the body—of the pain that the body experiences. Attending a performance at the Grand Guignol is a self-inflicted sadistic exercise as Marquis de Sade–like tortures are recreated nightly in spectacles of cruelty. And audiences buy a ticket to watch—to view the limb-severing, the eye-gouging, the nipple-piercing. Spectators pay to experience the sexual titillation and the artistic adventure, never having to protect or save the helpless victim.

Certainly horror films exploit a similar voyeuristic gaze, but the film spectator's passivity is greater. A film may arouse feelings of disgust and revulsion, but the abstracted film denies the viewer's physical, kinesthetic relationship to the performer—the tortured. In the little auditorium where the participants enact their sinister violence a mere twenty feet from the audience, the question of why the audience does not avert its gaze, indeed run to the victim's rescue, is compelling. Watching these violent spectacles cultivates in the observer both anxiety and a certain *Schadenfreude*. Here horror and comedy meet, as each exploits the idea of the audience as passive voyeur, who, despite the lack of physical involvement in the action, is complicit in the harm done to the characters. And, to press the metaphor a little further, the pain enjoyed through this voyeuristic indulgence needs the salve of comedy, where the characters generally skirt the physical sensation of pain.

Like comedy, which has often been contextualized theoretically in connection with fertility rites, I would argue that there is an impulse toward life in these Grand Guignol death masques. While virulent violence is performed onstage, the act of sitting in the auditorium not only separates and protects the viewer from the tortures, but these voyeurs are placed among the living—becoming survivors, able to escape. As Bergson says in his essay "Laughter," it is hard to laugh in the privacy of an armchair; likewise, the sense of relief, as the audience exits onto the dark street, is heightened by fleeing together, leaving the death, the morbidity, behind.

Not only the comedies, however, but also the most violent and macabre plays performed on an evening's bill at Le Théâtre du Grand Guignol provoke laughter, raising the issue of the relationship between pain and comedy or, more specifically: How can gruesome violence veer toward the comic? Aristotle mentions comedy in the *Poetics* but denies that the ugly in the comic mask implies pain, seeing only the grotesque and ridiculous. Aristotle and Plato are each distrustful of laughter, couching this reaction as valuable if a social corrective. Platonic laughter, for example, is valued as a superior, distancing response to evil and human folly. At the Grand Guignol there is something too godless, hopeless, as Wilson and Hand state, too "morally erratic," for a utilitarian concept of humor to hold merit. In this context laughter is more appropriately aligned with those, like Thomas Hobbes, who see sadism in laughter. Grand Guignol laughter is implicitly self-congratulatory, which links it to what Hand and Wilson describe as "this theatre's striving for mimesis, not just in the verisimilitude of its sex and violence but in its attempt to reflect the crises of modern consciousness in a nihilistic universe."[13]

But laughter is a physiological response as well, much like the wacky tics viewed in Dr. Berton's play. Gaze in these plays of horror and humor is vital; the theatrical frame permits staring. The peepshow aspect of attending a performance at the Grand Guignol emphasizes titillation and fetishizes the body. The body at the Grand Guignol is tactile, visceral, corporeal, and can be displayed experiencing pain. Although the comedies veer away from the physical reality of pain, both genres inhabit the same universe in that the horror plays, like comedy, do not cultivate pathos. If they did, the horror scenario, like the comic scenario, would be unbearable. Instead, horror and humor meet at the Grand Guignol by forcing the viewer to look, perhaps askew but nevertheless unsympathetically, at the plight of the characters. In comedy and horror the worst excesses of the human animal are put on display, and little permission is given, during a performance, to contemplate a universe that allows such torment.

There is, undeniably, something primal about horror theatre—the urge to see physical pain exacted without poetic justice, without rational explanation; the pleasure of horror and humor defies logic and reason. Laughter and pain precede conscious thought. In *The Joke and Its Relation to the Unconscious* Freud argues that jokes, like dreams, satisfy our unconscious desires; pleasure derives from being released from social inhibitions and repressed instincts, whether sexual or violent. Freud's ideas are eerily like his contemporary, the Grand Guignol's greatest voice, Andre de Lorde, who writes in the preface to his *La galerie des monstres* (1928), we all are a potential monster, suppressing a "thousand hidden forces, a thousand strange desires, a thousand obscure dreams."[14] Despite focusing on pain and death, laughter and terror at the Grand Guignol remind performer and spectator alike what it means to feel alive.

Notes

1. Jean Aragny and Francis Neilson, "The Kiss of Blood," in *Grand-Guignol: The French Theatre of Horror,* ed. and trans. Richard J. Hand and Michael Wilson (Exeter: University of Exeter Press, 2006), 249–50. Hand and Wilson are two major scholars and translators of the form, responsible for providing most of the published English translations. Blood Brothers used their translation in their "An Evening of Grand Guignol Horror," Oct. 19–28, 2006, Seventy-eighth Street Theatre Lab, 236 West Seventy-eighth St. at Broadway, NYC.

2. Agnès Pierron, *Le Grand Guignol: Le théâtre des peurs de la Belle Époque* (Paris: Robert Laffont, 1995), xiii.

3. Two excellent studies on laughter and its relationship to the comic genre are Marcel Gutworth, *Laughing Matter: An Essay on the Comic* (Ithaca, NY: Cornell University Press, 1993); and John Morreall, *Taking Laughter Seriously* (New York: SUNY Press, 1983). Morreall organizes historical perspectives on laughter in three categories: the Superiority Theory, the Incongruity Theory, and the Relief Theory; each helps to explain laughter at the Grand Guignol and how laughter functions in both comedy and horror.

4. Richard J. Hand and Michael Wilson, "The Grand-Guignol: Aspects of Theory and Practice," www.grandguignol.com/tri_2.htm (accessed Nov. 15, 2007).

5. František Deák, "Theatre du Grand Guignol," *TDR* 18, no. 1 (March 1974): 42, http://links.jstor.org/sici?sici=00125962%28197403%2918%3A1%3C34%3ATDGG%3E2.0.CO%3B2-O (accessed Dec. 20, 2007).

6. Daniel Gerould, *Gallant and Libertine: Eighteenth Century French Divertissements and Parades* (New York: Performing Arts Journal Publications, 1983), 9.

7. Hand and Wilson, "The Grand-Guignol," www.grandguignol.com/tri_3.htm.

8. Mel Gordon, *The Grand Guignol: Theatre of Fear and Terror,* rev. ed. (New York: Da Capo Press, 1997), 8.

9. Deák, "Théâtre du Grand Guignol," 42–43.

10. René Berton, *Après Coup! . . . ou Tics,* in *Grand-Guignol: The French Theatre of Horror,* ed. and trans. Richard J. Hand and Michael Wilson (Exeter: University of Exeter Press, 2006), 143.

11. Ibid., 151.

12. Beth Rae Gordon, "From Charcot to Charlot: Unconscious Imitation and Spectatorship in French Cabaret and Early Cinema," *Critical Inquiry* 27, no. 3 (spring 2001): 516.

13. Hand and Wilson, "The Grand-Guignol," www.grandguignol.com/tri_4.htm.

14. Quoted at ibid. My translation from the original: *mille forces cachées, mille désirs éstranges [sic], mille aspirations obscures.*

When Satire More Than

Closed on Saturday Night

Henry Fielding and the Licensing Act of 1737

Steven Dedalus Burch

GEORGE S. KAUFMAN once famously defined satire as what closed Saturday night. This comment renders satire, among other comedic forms, to be uncommercial, not ready to support the weight and economic obligation of a mainstream comedy. Besides, satires become dated and irrelevant very quickly—hence, the warning to would-be producers and authors. In eighteenth-century England, however, Henry Fielding wrote satires that closed not only Saturday night but virtually everything within the London theatre.

In the 1730s, after some false starts, Fielding began to find his mature voice as a playwright, through literary burlesque and, only later, political satire. Burlesque, defined as an exaggerated parody of a literary form or style, had been around since the ancient Greek theatre of Aristophanes, especially his parodies of Euripides. (*Women Celebrating the Thesmophoria* [411 BCE] and *The Frogs* [405 BCE] are among the earliest burlesques.) Fielding began his career with a succession of burlesques on such topics as Shakespeare and heroic tragedy, neoclassicism, Italian opera, and Colley Cibber with such audience favorites as *The Tragedy of Tragedies; or, The Life and Death of Tom Thumb the Great* (1731), *The Welsh Opera* (1731), and *Covent-Garden Tragedy* (1732) and within a few short years could claim to be the most popular playwright in London.[1] These burlesques opened up in Fielding a channel for his anger at the banal, pretentious writing and musical fads of the day. But, more important, they were to provide him with a platform for his political revulsion at the open corruption of the court of George II, his chief minister Robert Walpole, and the Parliament.

Robert Walpole, who had become Fielding's chief opponent and sa-

tirical target, had become the first Lord of the Treasury and Chancel-
lor of the Exchequer under George I, a position he maintained when
George II ascended to the throne. He quickly became the king's favorite and, subsequently, the most powerful and influential of the king's
ministers. In point of fact, most historians date the birth of the modern
British prime minister to Walpole's administration.

Throughout his ministry, which lasted more than two decades, Walpole exercised extraordinary cunning in his manipulation of the House
of Commons, exerting a profound influence on the structure of eighteenth-century politics. But that cunning was seriously undermined by
his open and blatant use of patronage and even outright bribery in maintaining his political power. His opposition included many writers of the
day, and several, including Fielding, wrote for the opposition newspaper,
The Craftsman. These writers scathingly lampooned Walpole's ministry
in pamphlets, ballads, and newspapers, helping to bring about a complete and utter contempt by the public toward Parliament and politics.

In 1736 Fielding wrote a five-act masterpiece of inspired, sustained
comic invective, *Pasquin*, and it was a box-office and critical sensation.
So much so that Fielding was encouraged to pursue a newer, looser form
of writing, merging the literary burlesque he had recently mastered, especially in *The Tragedy of Tragedies*, with a scattershot satirical approach
to the politics and culture of England. Sadly, the result of Fielding's
growth as a dramatist helped to bring about the Licensing Act of 1737,
which abruptly terminated his career in the theatre. The effects of the
Licensing Act have been well documented and will only be summarized
here. Leading up to that summary, this essay will look at three of Fielding's last plays, beginning with *Pasquin* (1736) and then turning to *The
Historical Register of 1736* and *Eurydice Hiss'd* (both 1737) and examine
how Fielding blends burlesque with topical satire in addition to breaking new ground in the drama.[2]

Pasquin

Pasquin is a rehearsal play of the type established by George Villiers in
his *The Rehearsal* (1671). In *The Rehearsal* we watch the ego-inflated author, Mr. Bayes, rehearse a company of actors in his new play as invited
guests observe. "As Bayes screams directions and simpers foolishly to his
guests, the poor players stumble through their parts."[3] By the play's end
there have been so many mishaps the guests have sneaked away and the
actors are "ready for mutiny" (ibid.). While there is much biting satire
of the theatre, and it is generally acknowledged that Villiers's play killed
off the entire form of the heroic tragedy, the focus of the play was the

inflated writing style of John Dryden, especially his *The Conquest of Granada*. In *Pasquin* Fielding uses the theatrical rehearsal as a venue from which to take off and go after a multitude of targets, both literary and nonliterary, for his indignant, malicious wit.

Fielding advertised his play as "By the Great Mogul's Company of English Comedians, Newly Imported . . . The Cloaths are old, but the Jokes intirely new."[4] He had recently taken over at the New Haymarket, an unlicensed theatre, as an impresario, referring to himself as the "Great Mogul," and formed his own company in which to perform the kind of theatre he cared passionately about. Fielding was intensely patriotic, and in play after play of his we find sharp verbal jabs at the importation of foreign culture, especially Italian opera and its singers (most notably the famed castrati Farinelli, adored by London high society, ridiculed as Fairbelly in *Pasquin*).

In *Pasquin* Fielding goes Villiers's play one better: he presents two plays in rehearsal. The first is a farce by Trapwit called *The Election;* the second is a tragedy by Fustian, *The Life and Death of Common-Sense*. In both, he sends up the Bayes-type playwright, by now a familiar figure of fun. Trapwit and Fustian are both extremely full of themselves and, underneath the inane polite chatter and fawning flattery, have no regard for the other's work. At the play's beginning Fielding presents us with a group of actors milling about and complaining about their late rehearsals (in Fielding's rehearsal plays the actors are always complaining). Fustian arrives, ready to rehearse his tragedy, but one of the actors is indisposed. Trapwit arrives even later, after we have been informed that he had been arrested for nonpayment of a bill. After many polite bows, Fustian implores Trapwit to begin his rehearsal first.

Trapwit's play, *The Election,* begins on the eve of an election, and we are shown the candidates of both parties (Whigs and Tories) as they court votes among the town's mayor and aldermen. The courting is by bribery. The court candidates, Lord Place and Colonel Promise, shower the mayor and aldermen with cash. The country candidates, Sir Henry Foxchase and Squire Tankard, bribe through gifts and business brought to town, all the while decrying those who would openly bribe with cash. Donald Thomas writes, "The audience filled the Little Theatre night after night to hear Mr. Trapwit directing his players in bribery, as though it were one of the most exalted arts in human history. . . . The play exploited and magnified a public weariness of political parties and the cynicism was widespread."[5]

In 1736 the target of this satire was unmistakable: Walpole was well-known for his ability to buy politicians, and the corruption of the court was an open secret. Also the Whigs, though they were the dominant party, were factionalized into court and country politicians. In *The Election*, after the town officials have been bribed by both parties, the court candidates then pursue power through the mayor's wife and daughter by promising them places in court. So keen is she of being at court that Mrs. Mayoress even agrees with Lord Place ("every one is keeps and is kept; there are no such things as marriages now-a-days") that her daughter's virtue is salable:

MISS MAYORESS. But must I go into keeping, mamma?
MRS. MAYORESS. Child, you must do what's in fashion.
MISS MAYORESS. But I have heard that's a naughty thing.
MRS. MAYORESS. That can't be, if your betters do it; people are punished for doing naughty things; but people of quality are never punished; therefore they never do any naughty things.[6]

Later, Place attempts to bribe a voter with another position at court:

2ND VOTER. I am a devilish lover of sack.
LORD PLACE. Sack, say you? . . . you shall be poet-laureate. (ibid., 184)

After this two-line swipe at Walpole and Colley Cibber, Trapwit sets up a familial conflict with the mayor, leaning toward Foxchase while his family is determined to support Lord Place.

Fielding has great fun with the neoclassicists and other academics about the rules governing playwriting. When, interrupting the action, Fustian asks Trapwit about the moral of his play, Trapwit replies, "I really will not tell you. . . . [S]ince you cannot find that out, I'll try whether you can find out the plot" (ibid., 187). At the play's end, in accordance with the "rules" of comedy, Trapwit contrives a sudden love affair between Miss Mayoress and Colonel Promise. After a prolonged comical silence of looks between the two, they speak of their love for one another, and she begs his forgiveness for her behavior. Both apoplectic and befuddled, Fustian demands of Trapwit how this can be since neither character had been seen onstage with the other. Indeed, this is the first time they have spoken to one another. Not so, replies Trapwit, they had spoken to one another offstage. He continues, "[W]ould you have everything brought upon the stage? I intend to bring ours to the dignity of the French stage. . . . [T]he French, you know, banish all cruelty from the stage; and I don't see why we should bring on a lady in ours, practicing all manner of cruelty upon her lover" (ibid., 197). In a final jest Trapwit's marriage unites all the rival political factions.

In act 3 Fielding introduces Sneerwell, a critic who arrives only in time to catch Trapwit's act 5 and who therefore understands nothing of what he sees. By act 4, as Fustian is about to begin his rehearsal, Trapwit finds a convenient excuse to not watch it and sneaks out of the theatre, leaving Sneerwell to make his fatuous remarks throughout the play.

The Life and Death of Common-Sense is an allegory about the overthrow of Queen Common-Sense by Queen Ignorance. Fielding begins by showing Fustian ridiculously defending his flattering dedication to his patron, insisting that he has used no flattery: "I abhor the least imputation of flattery. . . . [O]nly [your Lordship] give me leave to say, that you have more wit, sense, learning, honor, and humanity than all mankind put together" (ibid., 201). By playing up Fustian as buffoonish and somewhat hypocritical, Fielding gives himself the distance needed to target his enemies in Fustian's tragedy.

In this second play-within-a-play Fielding sets up Law, Religion (in the character of Firebrand), and Medicine (as Physic) as seeking to escape the "lethargic sway of Common-sense" (ibid., 206). Firebrand declares himself an enemy to Common-Sense and requests Law to assist him in enlarging the worship of the Sun. Queen Common-Sense then enters and upbraids Law for allowing those who are poor to go unredressed in their grievances. Word suddenly comes that Queen Ignorance has invaded the realm with an army from Italy and France of singers, fiddlers, tumblers, and rope-dancers. The climax of Fustian's tragedy is the face-off between the two queens. Ignorance claims Common-Sense's subjects complain that Common-Sense imposes a tax of thought, "for thinking only makes men wretched" (ibid., 219). At this point Firebrand stabs Common-Sense, and she dies. But she comes back as a ghost to haunt her subjects, and Ignorance and the others run offstage screaming with fright. The play-within-a-play, as well as the play itself, ends with the Ghost of Common-Sense giving the epilogue.

Pasquin was the smash hit of the season, running for more than sixty performances, rivaling the earlier success of *The Beggar's Opera*. All of London was talking about *Pasquin* and clearly loving it, satirical thrusts notwithstanding.[7] Goldgar suggests that it is twentieth-century critics who have elevated *Pasquin*'s standing as satire: "there is really little evidence to suggest that *Pasquin* was regarded as the daring political satire it is now said to be, much less a stepping stone toward the Licensing Act."[8] Robert Hume rebuts this, however: "Fielding provides a steady flow of local and topical allusions. . . . [T]hough he intermixes some innuendoes . . . he is careful never to force the audience to make hostile identifications. The play quite clearly says that England is politically corrupt and culturally degenerate, but the message is conveyed in a roundabout way and softened by theatrical high jinks. . . . *Pasquin* manages to be funny, boisterous, pointed, subtle and highly effective."[9]

The success of *Pasquin* encouraged Fielding to go further, in both his pointed commentary and in his groundbreaking merging of literary burlesque with satire. His next play was a minor afterpiece, *Tumble-Down Dick* (1736); it, too, was a success, especially as it played following *Pasquin*. But Fielding was saving up for his next attack, which would be even more stinging, grander, and revolutionary.

The Historical Register of 1736

As he did in *Pasquin,* Fielding opens with a rehearsal: actors milling about, complaining about their parts, and waiting for the author/director to show so that they may begin. Before the author arrives, a critic, Sourwit, and a patron, Lord Dapper, enter. On their inquiries they are informed by the actors that the piece cannot be typed as a comedy or a tragedy. Finally the author, Medley, shows and explains to his audience the intent of the piece and its irregular structure. Sourwit questions how the author can get the actions of an entire year into twenty-four hours (to satisfy the French neoclassical ideal). Fielding/Medley retorts, "[I]f I comprise the whole actions of the year in half an hour, will you blame me, or those who have done so little in that time?"[10] When Sourwit asks if the play's components "conduce to the main design" and what they are, Medley's answer is yes, the main design being "to divert the town and bring full houses" (ibid., 242). Clearly Fielding is setting up his audience not to expect a traditionally structured play. And he does not disappoint.

In fact, what Fielding did give his audience was a metatheatrical play that by postmodern standards seems to approach the anarchic spirit of such twentieth-century topical satire/reviews as *The Goon Show* and *Monty Python's Flying Circus. The Historical Register* is made up of six skits that are only connected tangentially, "unhampered by the constraints of plot and character development."[11] In fact, biographer Ronald Paulson argues that *The Historical Register* "[sums] up the strands that have developed in Fielding's plays over the last several years, all of which tended toward the genre of satire, and the metaphor of life as theatre."[12] Fielding might as well have titled his play *Scenes from London Life*. After opening with a thoroughly banal "Ode to the New Year" (a ripe parody of the trite odes being composed by England's then poet laureate/playwright Colley Cibber), Medley sets his first scene in a meeting of the political ministers of Corsica.[13]

As the scene is about to start, Sourwit spots a problem with Medley's play. "Here's a mistake in the print. . . . I observe the second politician is the first person who speaks." Medley replies patiently, "Sir, my first and greatest politician never speaks at all. . . . [T]he chief art of a politician is to keep a secret."[14] Medley then plunges into the politicians' debate, which consists of two items: the Turks and money. As to the first, no one seems to know anything that is happening. After much hemming the Fifth Politician speaks the primary line: "Hang foreign affairs, let us apply ourselves to money" (245), a line that Medley has his actors repeat with emphasis. They next debate how to get it. A tax is agreed upon. But what to tax? Learning, someone suggests. But the Third Politician complains that learning is only a "property of but a very few" and agrees to tax ignorance instead as it "will take in most of the great fortunes in the kingdom" (246).

This scene ends, and Medley turns to his audience and explains this scene was "the full account of the whole history of Europe" (246). The next satiric target is a council of society ladies in London, where Fielding indulges in one of his favorite japes, Italian opera and the immensely popular castrati singer Farinelli (here called Farinello). After his brief ridicule of society's culture vultures, Fielding then sweeps us into his pièce de résistance: the Society Auction.

This third skit of Fielding's is set in an auction house and is based on the fashionable auction sales conducted by Christopher Cock, which were always well attended by the beau monde. In *The Historical Register* the auctioneer has been rechristened Christopher Hen (and was played by Charlotte Charke, Colley Cibber's estranged daughter, who specialized in transgendered roles), and the auction consists of "such things as were never sold in any auction before" (251). Among the items on Hen's auction block are a "most curious remnant of Political Honesty . . . [a] most delicate piece of Patriotism . . . three grains of modesty . . . one bottle of Courage . . . all the Wit lately belonging to [a] composer of entertainments for the play-houses . . . a very clear Conscience . . . a very considerable quantity of Interest at Court . . . all the Cardinal Virtues . . . a great deal of Wit and a little Common Sense" (253–56). As each item is put up for sale, the bidders comment, and Fielding makes quite clear that each is considered of no great worth, except the item listed as Interest at Court, which is sold for one thousand pounds.[15] In the end, in an echo from *Pasquin,* Common-Sense does not get sold, as no one is interested.

The fourth episode interrupts the action with the arrival of Pistol exclaiming with great bluster (in a caricature of Theophilus Cobber) and allowing Fielding to deflate the artistic pretensions of the Cibbers, father and son. This target is carried into the fifth skit, which presents Apollo in a dialogue with Ground-Ivy, Pistol's father, about Ground-Ivy's rewriting of Shakespeare's texts.[16]

The sixth skit, with which Fielding ends his play, is the most damning against Walpole and his government. Four false Patriots are presented, and all are bribed by Quidam to do his bidding, and all for gold. At the end he has the Patriots dancing off the stage and losing their bribes through holes in their pockets. Quidam sweeps up and regains "so not to lose one halfpenny by his generosity; so far from it, that he will get his wine for nothing, and the poor people, alas! out of their own pockets, pay the whole reckoning" (267).

Like *Pasquin, The Historical Register* was immediately and hugely successful. Its fiercely open hostility toward Walpole, as well as its radical extension of the "rehearsal technique,"[17] gave it a depth few other works possessed during this period. It also made Fielding a prime target of the government. In *Pasquin* his satire was solid and clearly aimed, but his anger was under control. As Donald Thomas writes, *Pasquin* and some of his earlier burlesques were seen as "schoolboy lampoons on the Prime Minister and his failings."[18] Now, however, his rage became too open to dismiss. Robert Hume writes, "Denying the acid factionalism . . . would be difficult. The bribes Quidam gives the false patriots in Act Three are not exactly a subtle comment on Walpole's modus operandi. . . . The work is devastatingly nasty about Walpole, and no minister benefits from being made to look both craven and crooked."[19] And Thomas points out that the audiences for *The Historical Register* were not only laughing; they were also applauding.[20]

Additionally, for those readers and viewers unable to determine Fielding's intended target, Fielding, in his published preface to the play, coyly leads his readers to the heart of his satire: "Who is this Quidam, that turns the patriots into ridicule, and bribes them out of their honesty? Who but the devil could act such a part? . . . Gold hath been always his favorite bait wherewith he fisheth for sinners. . . . Indeed it is so plain who is meant by this Quidam, that he who maketh any wrong application thereof, might as well mistake the name of Thomas for John, or old Nick for old Bob."[21] In an age when literally everyone, educated or not, would understand "old Nick" as one of Satan's nicknames, the joining of his name to Walpole's ("old Bob") was as blatant an attack as could be conceived. Walpole did not need any more ammunition to counterattack, but Fielding, on a roll, provided him with more, just the same.

Eurydice Hiss'd

The last play in this study came on the heels of the success of *The Historical Register*.[22] A one-act afterpiece, to play in concert with *The Historical Register, Eurydice Hiss'd* begins as another rehearsal play. Once

were sufficiently cowed by Fielding's silencing. Fielding was only thirty years old, and he never wrote another play.

Notes

1. Fielding was more popular than either Coffee or Carey, and "in terms of performances he was second only to Cibber among the authors of his era" (Brian McCrea, *Henry Fielding and the Politics of Mid-Eighteenth-Century England* [Athens: University of Georgia Press, 1982], 57).

2. Bertrand Goldgar cites *The Historical Register of 1736* as "Fielding's most open and unmistakable satire of Walpole" (Bertrand Goldgar, *Walpole and the Wits: The Relation of Politics to Literature, 1722–1742* [Lincoln: University of Nebraska Press, 1976], 151).

3. Brice Harris, ed., *Restoration Plays* (New York: Modern Library, 1953), viii.

4. *London Daily Post,* and *General Advertiser,* March 5, 1736.

5. Donald Thomas, *Henry Fielding* (London: Weidenfeld and Nicolson, 1990), 127.

6. Henry Fielding, *Complete Works: Plays and Poems,* vol. 4 (New York: Croscup and Sterling, 1902), 181.

7. Harold Pagliaro, *Henry Fielding: A Literary Life* (London: Macmillan, 1998), 104.

8. Goldgar, *Walpole and the Wits,* 153.

9. Robert Hume, *Henry Fielding and the London Theatre, 1728–1737* (Oxford: Clarendon Press, 1988), 213.

10. Fielding, *Complete Works,* 4:241.

11. Hume, *Henry Fielding and the London Theatre,* 235.

12. Ronald Paulson, *The Life of Henry Fielding: A Critical Biography* (Oxford: Blackwell, 2000), 67.

13. Obviously Fielding decided that topical, political satire would work best if he could present the events in a far-off country. Fielding, as Medley, in 1736 writes of Corsica as "the chief scene of politics of all Europe" (Fielding, *Complete Works,* 4:244). In one of history's lovely coincidences, in just six decades a Corsican would be at the center of all European politics: Bonaparte.

14. Fielding, *Complete Works,* 4:244.

15. A disgruntled bidder complains that "I know a shop where I can buy it for less" (ibid., 256). To Fielding's audience this was a very obvious jab at Walpole.

16. Colley Cibber had recently rewritten Shakespeare's *King John.* Fielding has Ground-Ivy proclaiming that "it was a maxim of mine, when I was at the head of theatrical affairs, that no play, though ever so good, would do without alteration" (ibid., 262).

17. Hume, *Henry Fielding and the London Theatre,* 234.

18. Donald Thomas, *Henry Fielding* (London: Weidenfeld and Nicolson, 1990), 132.

19. Hume, *Henry Fielding and the London Theatre*, 237.

20. Among those in the audience, laughing and, more important, applauding, was the heir to the British throne, the Prince of Wales. Thomas, *Henry Fielding*, 132.

21. Fielding, *Complete Works*, 4:236.

22. Although not technically the last play he ever wrote, *Eurydice Hiss'd* was the last play Fielding ever produced.

23. Fielding, *Complete Works*, 4:298.

24. Ibid., 299. Paulson, among many others, notes that Fielding had taken over the Little Haymarket Theatre, which offered him the "opportunity of an ad hoc situation of a sort that was ideal for his improvisational genius . . . in which he could try out not only his new plays, but those of others" (Paulson, *The Life of Henry Fielding*, 68).

25. Fielding, *Complete Works*, 4:301.

26. Hume, *Henry Fielding and the London Theatre*, 238.

27. Peter Lewis, *Fielding's Burlesque Drama* (Edinburgh: Edinburgh University Press, 1987), 195.

28. Ibid., 200–201.

29. Hume, *Henry Fielding and the London Theatre*, 243.

30. John Loftis, *The Politics of Drama in Augustan England* (Oxford: Clarendon Press, 1963), 140.

31. Thomas, *Henry Fielding*, 134. Loftis also dismisses this suggestion and argues it unlikely that Fielding would have composed "such a coarsely vulgar piece" (Loftis, *The Politics of Drama in Augustan England*, 141).

32. Pagliaro, *Henry Fielding*, 112.

33. See Jeremy Collier, "A Short View of the Immorality and Profaneness of the English Stage," in *Dramatic Theory and Criticism: Greeks to Grotowski*, ed. Bernard F. Dukore (Orlando: Harcourt Brace Jovanovich, 1974), 351–58.

34. Hume, *Henry Fielding and the London Theatre*, 248.

35. This is still a point of contention among historians. Loftis (*The Politics of Drama in Augustan England*, 139) and Goldgar (*Walpole and the Wits*, 156) argue that Fielding was not responsible for the Licensing Act, and others have also taken up that refrain.

Meat, Bones, and Laughter without Words

Finding Bergson's *Laughter* in Beckett's *Act without Words I*

Christopher Morrison

A FEW YEARS after Samuel Beckett rose to international fame with *Waiting for Godot*,[1] Ruby Cohn wrote in *Samuel Beckett: The Comic Gamut*: "Since Bergson in *Le rire* bases his analysis of the comic largely on the comedy of manners, it is not surprising that his framework best fits this Beckett book. Of the three domains, situation, character, and language, it is mainly upon the last that Beckett's comic effects depend." In her analysis of early Beckett works, Cohn finds evidence to back up this assertion: "Bergson's linguistic breakdown is almost sufficient to explain the comic of *More Pricks*." Of Part III of *Watt*, she writes, "Beckett avails himself of certain Bergsonian comic linguistic tools . . . [and] makes use of Bergson's favorite example of linguistic ambiguity, the pun." Yet, as Cohn moves toward the late 1940s to discuss Beckett's more mature works—his "first burst into French"— she finds that "the Bergsonian comic roster virtually disappears."[2]

And from that page and year forward, 1962, any serious scholarly discussion of the influence of Bergson on Beckett also virtually disappears. A look at the relevant entry in *The Grove Companion to Samuel Beckett* suggests why. At first the editors, C. J. Ackerley and S. E. Gontarski, acknowledge that Bergson's taking of Descartes' famous *Je suis une chose qui pense,* and substituting his own *Je suis une chose qui dure* "[asserts] the primacy within consciousness of duration. This would be central to [Beckett's] thought." In the end, however, Ackerley and Gontarski dismiss Bergson: "[A]ttempts to associate SB with Bergson founder on one rocky reef: SB's total rejection of vitalism."[3]

Despite Cohn's assertion that Bergson was concerned mainly with text, and despite the general passing over of Bergson's theories by Beckett scholars, an understanding of *Laughter (Le rire)*[4] in combination with *la durée* is—at the very least—an important critical tool for a director of Beckett approaching the entirely pantomimed *Act without Words I.*[5] To explore this thesis I will (1) provide an overview of salient aspects of Bergson and his philosophy; (2) connect him to Beckett; (3) point out some salient points in *Laughter;* (4) apply it to *Act without Words I;* and (5) use what I have shown as a heuristic to comment on the directorial choices in the *Beckett on Film* 2001 version of the play by the Czech director Karel Reisz.

In the years following the publication in Paris of the French philosopher and Nobel Laureate Henri Bergson's *L'Evolution créatrice* (1907), and particularly its English translation *Creative Evolution* (1911),[6] Bergson's theories of "duration" *(la durée)* and *l'élan vital,* which dealt with the value of inner contemplation and intuition, in A. F. Losev's words, "resounded throughout the world." Richard Lehan goes further: "Bergson's influence, direct or indirect, on modern literature cannot be denied or de-emphasized. . . . [T]he Bergsonian construct generated a realm of discourse from which modernism, as a literary movement, was inseparable." Writers such as T. S. Eliot attended Bergson's lectures at the Sorbonne, fell under the spell of "the first philosopher to take Time seriously," and were enchanted by the revitalization of the role of intuition promulgated in Bergson's writings and teachings. Only a decade or so later, the philosopher's reputation had declined to the extent that detractors began to refer to Bergsonianism derogatorily as the "time-cult." Yet writers such as Marcel Proust, William Faulkner, Ernest Hemingway, and Robert Frost, psychologists such as Jean Piaget, and the French existentialist movement of Jean-Paul Sartre and Albert Camus all owe a considerable debt to the man of whom Wyndham Lewis wrote in 1927, "more than any other single figure [he] is responsible for the main intellectual characteristics of the world we live in."[7]

As Anthony Uhlmann has shown, Samuel Beckett made use of Bergson's philosophy in his movie *Film* to develop ideas about the image and "its relationship to thought."[8] But what influence did *la durée* and *l'élan vital* have on the Irish author and playwright, perhaps the only native English-speaking absurdist to have written in Bergson's native language and country? In particular, what elements of Bergson's *Le rire* can we find embedded in *Act without Words I?*

The ideas promulgated in *Le rire* are predicated on an understanding of *la durée.* The latter came at a time of transition in philosophical theories of the mind. Late nineteenth-century artists faced a universe seen by most philosophers as purely mechanistic and predetermined. Human beings were born into this mechanical universe, and within it they could act only according to laws and conditions laid down in the past. Anything an artist "created" was, in fact, preordained. What might have felt like "inspiration" was no more than a pretentious word for something that the artist, subject to the rigid but intricate laws of cause and effect, could never have escaped from "creating." This philosophical "straightjacket" took the "fun"—the egotistical satisfaction—of creative intuition away from artists. Where was the role of God or Divine (or Human) Inspiration? Even Charles Darwin, who did so much to remove the hand of God from the evolutionary equation, felt a great loss of aesthetic sensibilities as a result of his own discoveries: "My mind seems to have become a kind of machine for grinding laws out of large collections of facts. It sometimes makes me hate science."[9]

As the nineteenth century drew to a close, however, this view of the universe began to fall apart under the weight of new scientific discoveries. As Fink observed, "Beginning in 1895–96 with the discovery of X-rays and radioactivity, and continuing with the development of the quantum theory, the new physics 'chipped away at the classical picture of a static universe composed of fixed and permanent atoms and molecules. . . . A nondeterminist physics was gradually taking shape which created significant doubts about mechanical causation and which therefore struck at the heart of mechanistic science.'" This led to writers such as Virginia Woolf taking a greater interest in the psychological, irrational nature of human beings. "Life is not a series of gig-lamps symmetrically arranged; life is a luminous halo, a semi-transparent envelope surrounding us from the beginning of consciousness to the end."[10]

By the time *L'Evolution créatrice* appeared in 1907, Bergson (1859–1941) had established a respected career as a philosopher. His insight was that evolution of the mind had an element of spontaneity or vital spirit *(l'élan vital)* that did *not* lie within the realm of empirically predetermined physical laws. From his study of Darwin Bergson found that *l'élan vital* existed outside of "normal" time and normal physics. These properties, intrinsic only to natural and psychological dynamic processes, set *l'élan vital* apart explanatorily and ontologically from the predetermined dynamics of inert matter in Newtonian mechanics. In one leap, therefore, Bergson gave back to artists of all kinds the ownership of a creative spark. And not just artists: "He naturalizes the saint, the artist and the prophet. These stand at junctions of openness and freshness." This idea excited artists around Europe. For example, the idea melded seamlessly into the deep-rooted intuitionism of Russian Orthodoxy. "Many Russian modernists turned to Bergsonian intuition [. . .] as [a weapon] against [. . .] the materialism of Marxist-Leninism. At the same time, they spiritualized Bergson's secular ideas in accord with their inherently religious/theurgic impulse to uncover divine reality." William James, elder brother of Henry, whose own theory of stream of consciousness anticipated Bergson's ideas, put it more poetically: "open Bergson and new horizons loom on every page you read. It is like the breath of the morning and the song of birds. It tells of reality itself."[11]

Intuition, the act of mind that grasps *l'élan vital* directly, and does not either analyze it logically into atomic moments or assimilate it to static "spatial" shapes or structures, arose from Bergson's scrutiny of consciousness and his concept of *la durée*. His theory starts out sounding entirely Jamesian: "I find, first of all, that I pass from state to state. I am warm or cold, I am merry or sad, I work or I do nothing, I look at what is around me or I think of something else. Sensations, feelings, volitions, ideas—such are the changes into which my existence is divided and which color it in turns." Bergson points out that others who have thought about awareness tend to think that what he has just described involves a series of switches from a *static* state, of, say, "boredom," to another *static* state of, say, "excitement." Bergson finds that, in fact, all states are "undergoing change every moment: if a mental state ceased to vary, its duration would cease to flow."[12]

Bergson then moves to the function of memory. While others have tended to think of memory as a way of filing ideas into more or less easily retrievable boxes to which we return later to access the discrete idea, scene, sound, and so forth, Bergson says that memory is made of something different: *la durée*. This is a rolling wave constantly nibbling away at the present. "My mental state, as it advances on the road of time, is continually swelling with the duration which it accumulates; it goes on increasing—rolling upon itself as a snowball on snow."[13] Thus, even when we gaze on an unchanging object, the nature of our experience is modified over time because the previous experience of the object is added into the swelling wave of memory.

Should someone object to this idea of constant change by suggesting that this is not how our consciousness appears to us, Bergson replies that we only *notice*, that is to say, *apply our intellect*—which is separate from the process he is describing—*intermittently*. "The apparent discontinuity of the psychical life is then due to our attention being fixed on it by a series of separate acts. . . . A thousand incidents arise, which seem to be cut off from those which precede them: . . . [T]hey are the beats of the drum which break forth here and there in a symphony." These drumbeats, acts of intellectual perception, form a sort of network— threaded on the "formless *ego*, indifferent and unchangeable" [Bergson's italics]—that obscures the constant roll of duration underneath.

This network is "an artificial imitation of the internal life." It was duration, the continuous progress of the past, which gnaws at the present and grows into the future and swells as it grows, that became the model for modernist writers' inner dialogue.[14]

Samuel Beckett (1906–89) was still a five-year-old child, growing up in Dublin, when *Creative Evolution* was first published. After he graduated from Trinity College, majoring in French and Italian, he got a prestigious position teaching English at the *Ecole Normale Supérieure* in Paris from 1928 to 1930. Bergson had been a student there (1878–81) and taught there from 1897 to 1900. The year before Beckett arrived, Bergson received the Nobel Prize for Literature.

Two compelling sources of direct evidence of Beckett's close understanding of Bergson arise in 1931 when Beckett was back in Dublin teaching at Trinity College. That spring he made his only recorded appearance as an actor, appearing in an adaptation of Corneille's *Le cid* called *Le Kid*. Beckett had no role as a writer in this. Yet because of the element that time played in the much rewritten and slapstick script, Beckett wrote to a friend using English, Italian, Irish, and French vocabulary and tacking on the end a cryptic parenthetical suggesting that Bergson's ideas were common currency between them: "This *vitaccia* is *terne* (dull) beyond all belief. . . . [W]e gave 3 plays at the Peacock—*La Quema, Souriante Mme Beudet* and *Le Kid* (Corneille and Bergson)."[15]

A diligent student in Beckett's Trinity College lectures provides confirmation that Beckett had absorbed Bergson. Anthony Uhlmann writes, "During the Michaelmas term of 1931 Beckett taught a course on Gide and Racine . . . and notes to these lectures, taken by Rachel Burrows, have survived. Parts of these explicitly touch upon Beckett's understanding of Bergson's concept of intuition, and its influence on art and literature in France."[16] (I have suggested elsewhere that the two tramps in *Godot* are stuck in a Bergsonian limbo, what the philosopher would call a "permanent present," and their only way out is for Godot, who represents the immediate future, to appear.)[17]

While the short book covers many art forms, the main argument of *Laughter: An Essay on the Meaning of the Comic*, first published in 1900, is that comedy functions as a mechanism of social correction and that human beings are comic whenever they ignore *la durée* and allow themselves or part of themselves to become absentminded in body or mind. The latter represents humans acting in some ways like a machine. To give a simple example,[18] a man would "lose grace" in the Bergsonian sense when he forgets to cut or comb his hair. Walking around with his hair wild and woolly, the man would seem comic to fellow members of society. They would consequently laugh/snigger/point at the unkempt individual, thus setting in motion the socially useful aspect of comedy. The amusement alerts the woolly-headed butt of the laughter to the element of his (in this case) body that suggests "something mechanical encrusted on the living."[19] Alerted to the particular way in which he has become a little like a machine, the butt can respond, readjust, and bring to an end the absentminded behavior—in this example, get a haircut and/or comb his hair. Thus he (a) returns to the state of grace offered by paying attention to *la durée* and (b) more importantly, practically, and obviously rejoins the accepted norm of his society—people with neat, short hair. Of course, as virtually no one in the world is aware of this mechanism, the entire process takes place at the level of intuition.

Beckett has no interest in the "utility" of these ideas. Vivian Mercier, in his book *Beckett/Beckett*, acknowledges that Beckett "has caught a glimpse of many a philosophic theory," and Mercier argues that philosophy *does* inform much of Beckett's works but in a very specific—if not singular—way. "[Beckett] once confessed, 'I take no sides. I am interested in the shape of ideas. There is a wonderful sentence in Augustine: "Do not despair; one of the thieves was saved. Do not presume; one of the thieves was damned." That sentence has a wonderful shape. It is the *shape* that matters'"[20] (italics added). Mercier continues: "[Beckett] loves to take philosophic wisdom in its tritest, most abstract form . . . and to flesh it out with the minute particularity indispensable to art." As an example, Mercier discusses the screenplay for Beckett's only big-screen movie, *Film*. He quotes the opening words, which come under the heading "General":

—Esse est percipi.
—All extraneous perceptions suppressed, animal, human, divine, self-perception maintains in being.
—Search of non-being in flight from extraneous perception breaking down in inescapability of self-perception.[21]

So far, the reader may reasonably conclude that the subsequent screenplay will promulgate or at least grapple with the validity of Berkley's dictum, *Esse est percipi* (To be is to be perceived). The next line of the screenplay brutally kicks this conclusion aside: "—No truth value attached to above, regarded as of merely structural and dramatic convenience."

Similarly, Beckett uses Bergson's ideas in *Laughter* purely structurally and dramatically; it is their *shape*—perhaps even the *pattern* of their words on the page—that matters, not their intrinsic truth or lack thereof. Beckett doesn't care about any "social use" of his plays. Nor is he attempting to get a laugh. He is just using abstractions from Bergson's *Laughter* (predicated on an understanding of *la durée*) to "flesh . . . out . . . the minute particularity indispensable to art."

What are these "abstractions"? In chapter 1 of *Laughter* Bergson discusses three manifestations of the comic in "something mechanical encrusted on the living." The third of these is *"We laugh every time a person gives us the impression of being a thing"* (Bergson's italics). "We laugh at Sancho Panza tumbled into a bed-quilt and tossed into the air like a football. We laugh at Baron Munchausen turned into a cannon-ball and travelling through space. But certain tricks of circus clowns might afford a still more precise exemplification of the same law." He continues:

> On two occasions only have I observed this style of the comic in its unadulterated state. . . . The first time, the clowns came and went, collided, fell and jumped up and down in a uniformly accelerated rhythm. . . . And it was more and more to the jumping up again, the *redound*, that the attention of the public was attracted. Gradually, one lost sight of the fact that they were men of flesh and blood like ourselves.

If we combine this effect with Bergson's repeated mention of the idea of the human acting like a puppet, and the idea that "a really living life should never repeat itself," leading to his conclusion that human repetition is intrinsically comic, we begin to see any human being redounding repeatedly (in a public setting) with no apparent reason as a paradigm of Bergsonian pantomimic comedy.[22]

In the first part of chapter 2, "The Comic Element in Situations," Bergson describes three kinds of common comic situations: "The Jack-in-the-box," "The Dancing-jack," and "The Snow-ball."[23] Of the dancing-jack, Bergson writes, "There are innumerable comedies in which one of the characters thinks he is speaking and acting freely, and consequently, retains all the essentials of life, whereas, viewed from a certain standpoint, he appears as a mere toy in the hands of another, who is playing with him." Bergson continues: "All that is serious in life comes from our freedom. . . . What, then, is requisite to transform all this [freedom] into a comedy? Merely to fancy that our seeming freedom conceals the strings of a dancing-jack, and that we are, as the poet says, 'humble marionettes / The wires of which are pulled by Fate.'" The "snow-ball," as we will see, represents the most obvious "shape" that I believe stimulated Beckett in writing *Act*. Bergson writes here of "a mental diagram, [an] abstract formula," of which "the rolling snow-ball, which increases in size as it moves along," is an example. The circumstances are all different, but "they suggest the same abstract vision, that an effect which grows by arithmetical progression, so that the cause, insignificant at the outset, culminates by a necessary evolution in a result as important as it is unexpected." He describes one of these, which "is employed rather frequently. . . . [A] certain thing, say a letter, happens to be of supreme importance to a certain person and must be recovered at all costs. This thing which always vanishes just when you think you have caught it, pervades the entire play, 'rolling up' increasingly serious and unexpected incidents as it proceeds."[24]

I have given a representative selection of the content of *Laughter* that can be applied to *Act*. Let us turn to the dramaticule itself. Beckett wrote it in French as "Acte sans paroles 1" in 1956 for the dancer Deryk Mendel. Consisting of just four pages of stage directions, the play debuted at the Royal Court with music by Beckett's cousin John Beckett. Beckett's English version, which I will use, was published with the subtitle "A mime for one player" alongside *Endgame* two years later.

Briefly, a "man" is flung backward onto a stage lit as though a "desert," with "Dazzling light." He falls, gets up immediately, and after some actions goes off. This is repeated twice. For the rest of the play he is onstage interacting with various props: a "little tree," a pair of tailor's scissors, a "tiny carafe" labeled "Water," some cubes on which he stands, a lasso. The play ends after some fifteen minutes with the man "lying on his side, his face toward the auditorium, staring before him" as some of the props seem to try to tempt him to further reaction.[25]

Beckett described this "man" as "just 'human meat—or bones.'"[26] This small piece of evidence alone points to something Bergsonian. While he is not straightforwardly the "machine encrusted on the living," the man represents the *living*—in the sense of "sentience"—*removed* from the human being: the heart beats, the limbs move, and the autonomic system required to regulate these behaviors functions. The result of this process is the exposure of the underlying machine in the man— and Man—which, by Bergsonian definition, would be the comic "encrustation" that has accumulated in his life. Furthermore, if Beckett's "bones" option is adopted (rather than "meat"), we have the classic skeletal puppets. These can only be moved by strings attached to limbs in the fashion of the "humble marionettes, the wires of which are pulled by Fate."

The redounding clowns that Bergson enjoyed so much also seemed to act as mere meat and bones. At first glance this statement appears to contradict Bergson's observation that, as they repeatedly redounded, "one lost sight of the fact that [the clowns] were men of flesh and blood like ourselves." Yet, of course, Bergson is confirming that the clowns *are* made of flesh and blood/meat and bones. It is merely our *perception* of them that changes as they become more machinelike to the "comic sensors," if you will, in our eyes and brain. We have arrived at the point where, crucially, Beckett ignores the central comic interpretation of Bergson; we have located the "rocky reef" of Beckett's "total rejection" of Bergsonian vitalism. For the philosopher the comic effect is produced in the observer when he or she "experiences" something machinelike in the human object. Bergson continues: "[As the clowns continued to redound,] one began to think of bundles of all sorts, falling and knocking against each other. Then the vision assumed a more definite aspect. The forms grew rounder, the bodies rolled together and seemed to pick themselves up like balls. Then at last appeared the image toward which the whole of this scene had doubtless been unconsciously evolving—large rubber balls hurled against one another in every direction."[27]

Beckett, however, has no interest in "vision," this internalized layer of added perceptions. He has merely borrowed the "shape" of part of Bergson's writing, the narrative externalities, and adapted them to his own needs, writing the exact movements the actor is to perform with no intention that anything "comic" should emerge. And there is considerable detail involved in the man's act of falling and getting up. It begins, "The man is flung backwards on stage from right wing. He falls." Consider the first example from real life that Bergson uses in *Laughter:* "A man, running along the street, stumbles and falls; the passers-by burst out laughing. They would not laugh at him, I imagine, could they suppose that the whim had suddenly seized him to sit down on the ground." It has been suggested that one might think of Beckett's agenda in *Act* as being to carry out actions mentioned by Bergson in *Laughter* while managing to avoid any comic interpretation. A man running onto the stage and falling would be mildly funny. Yet the stage directions make it clear ("flung backwards") that the man has no agency here in appearing onstage and therefore cannot be accused of clumsiness. In Bergson, though, "[t]hey laugh [at the man who has fallen while running down the street] because his sitting down is involuntary. Consequently, it is not his sudden change of attitude that raises a laugh, rather the involuntary element in this change, his clumsiness, in fact."[28]

A question that arises for the performer is whether the fall is caused by the act of being flung. The period before the statement "He falls" suggests that the two acts are not connected. If this is so, given the double circumstances of the man having no responsibility for arriving onstage and the fact that his falling is not connected to the act of arriving, these two acts and all those that follow become no more than movements performed by the meat and bones connected to a human autonomic system. No clumsiness can be attributed, so there can be no comic interpretation.

Can this entity experience duration? After the man falls, he "gets up immediately" (the redound), "dusts himself, turns aside, reflects." The man does not seek to return from whence he came or even to look back there. He does not observe his new circumstances; he immediately goes to this condition of reflection, as close as anyone can get to concentration on the inner flux of *la durée* without Beckett going into a detailed Bergsonian explanation. By implication—the whole sequence is repeated twice, and he often returns to this in the rest of the play—this is the man's default mode of existence. Beckett gives no indication anywhere of how long any of the actions in the script are expected to take. Everything exists outside time. In that sense these are "instant" stage directions, one might say—simply remove from packet and add Time to taste. Quite feasibly, if the director chose so, the performance could last for hours.

If the man's default mode is reflection, how does he move on? Again, entirely without any agency from himself: "Whistle from right wing." Although we cannot be sure that he has heard this sound, the man reflects more and then goes off toward the sound of the whistle. As I mentioned above in the discussion of *la durée*, Bergson argued that we only apply our intellect—which is separate from *la durée*—intermittently. "The apparent discontinuity of the psychical life is then due to our attention being fixed on it by a series of separate acts" of which these whistles may be one.

Once the man has done "reacting to" the whistle, he settles into an onstage "plot" closely derived from Bergson's "snow-ball": "This thing which vanishes just when you think you have caught it," which he said often provided the plot framework for a whole play. In *Act* a small tree descends from the flies with a single bough, a "meager tuft of palms," which casts a circle of light. The man sits down under the shade, a pair of tailor's scissors appears above him, and the tree folds up "like a parasol." Next a "tiny carafe, to which is attached a huge label inscribed 'Water,' descends from the flies." The following two pages, the middle 70 percent of the play, are concerned with the man's "efforts" (I use quotation marks here because the word *efforts* suggests volition on the part of the protagonist, which would be wrong to assume) to grasp the carafe. Note that the carafe is more the *notion* of water than any realistic amount that would slake his thirst. In any case we have no indication that the man is thirsty.

Here one thinks of Tantalus stretching for the grapes above him. The water comes close; the man reaches up; it "flies" further way. He puts the wooden blocks on the ground to help him reach, and it disappears completely. In discussing the situation where the attention is drawn to the "material side of the body," as opposed to the vital soul's "lightness and subtlety," Bergson writes: "Then the body will become to the soul . . . inert matter dumped down upon living energy. . . . And we shall experience it most strongly when we are shown the soul *tantalised* by the needs of the body" (Bergson's italics). All these actions are interspersed with his periods of reflection so that we seem to be watching a man whose natural state is concentration on his inner *élan vital* but who is constantly interrupted by intellectual "beats of a drum." Paradoxically, this is the point at which the piece most "risks" provoking laughter. We, the audience, have seen those same plays and movies. (Or perhaps, only those of us who have seen Laurel and Hardy movies and others of the era recognize the device.) But Beckett subverts any likelihood we have of laughing at the man by the introduction of a hint of suicidal thoughts. "He looks at his hands, looks round for scissors, sees them, goes and picks them up, starts to trim his nails, stops, reflects, runs his fingers along blade of scissors, goes and lays them on [a] small cube, turns aside, opens his collar, frees his neck and fingers it."[29] But even this is subverted by the "snow-ball." When he turns to pick up the scissors again, they have gone and along with them any method of suicide. Any comedic effect that the snowball had generated by its machinelike repetitions has been subverted by the inkling we get that this human-shaped pile of meat and bones has managed to come up with one idea: his extinction by his own hand.

The widespread availability of the film of *Act,* directed by Karel Reisz and featuring the Irish actor Sean Foley (in the boxed set of Beckett's works for theatre, *Beckett on Film*), provides a convenient example for experiencing in concrete form the theory discussed in this essay. Because it contains elements and actions not mentioned in Beckett's script, however, this filmic realization proves to be an easy target for almost any theoretically driven critique of the directorial choices. For example, the play is located in a realistic looking stretch of sandy desert complete with two kinds of insect noises and sand dunes. The man shouts in anger or fright at one point, looks wildly offstage from whence he has been shoved—as if expecting a monster to appear—and, later, pulls his sweater over his head because he finds the heat of the sun too much. Thus, when the palm tree appears behind him *after* this action, the environment has reacted to his desires. This implies an anthropocentric world, albeit one where the "snow-ball" is given its Bergsonian interpretation as a device for frustrating in a machinelike way the desires of the complete man.

From the point of view of this essay—that the work is Bergsonian in shape but not spirit—the most obvious problem with the Reisz film, beyond those mentioned above, is the complete omission of the periods of reflection. The man falls and scrambles up from the sand, and, because this man is a fully intellectualized human—with needs, fears, and strategies—he frantically looks off to see what dangers will arrive next. Consequently, for him to constantly turn aside and reflect would appear most unnatural. The result—and this applies to the entire film—is a psychologized, *la durée*-free travesty of Beckett's intentions.

The question remains as to why Bergson's influence on Beckett has been largely ignored since the 1960s. One reason, as we have seen, is that the connection between the two is highly idiosyncratic and therefore somewhat camouflaged. Despite the above Bergsonian analysis, *The Grove Companion* is correct: Beckett is not a vitalist. Two other sociopolitical reasons suggest themselves. First, *Laughter* contains some uncomfortable writing on skin color intermingled with class-based condescension: "And why does one laugh at a negro? . . . I rather fancy the correct answer was suggested to me one day in the street by an ordinary cabby, who applied the expression 'unwashed' to the negro fare he was driving."[30] In other words, Bergson is suggesting "we" would laugh at African Americans because they seem to have forgotten to wash. Second, Bergson's philosophies fell out of favor, and, until the last five or ten years, his works have been somewhat disregarded. While his philosophical ideas had already been superseded and had greatly faded from their apogee of popularity long before 1939—when the true nature of Hitler's ambitions became all too clear—commentators came to see Bergson's *la durée* as instrumental, along with the philosophies of Nietzsche, Sorel, and others, in giving Mussolini and Hitler philosophical legitimacy. Hence, some blame for the rise of fascism and the tumultuous wars that ensued came to be laid at Bergson's feet. In 1941, writing in the first edition of the Paris-based, clandestine review *La pensée libre,* Georges Politzer, who would himself be tortured and executed by the Nazis for his adherence to Communism, commented on the recent passing of Bergson: "In the German press . . . the death of Bergson served as an occasion for instructive commentary. . . . A first note . . . didn't mention the 'non-Aryan' character of Bergson and indicated in soothing tones that Bergsonian philosophy had worked for 'the preparation of the new world.'"[31] Bergson, a Jew who toward the end of his life leaned toward Catholicism, did not support the Nazis. But to be seen as contributing to the rationale for fascism is an indictment that may have left an indelible mark, a mark that may be more correctly deemed a stigma.

Notes

1. Samuel Beckett, *Waiting for Godot: A Tragicomedy in Two Acts* (New York: Grove, 1954).

2. Ruby Cohn, *Samuel Beckett: The Comic Gamut* (New Brunswick, NJ: Rutgers University Press, 1962), 22, 26, 72, 105.

3. C. J. Ackerley and S. E. Gontarski, eds., *The Grove Companion to Samuel Beckett* (New York: Grove, 2004), 49.

4. Henri Bergson, *Laughter: An Essay on the Meaning of the Comic,* trans. Cloudesley Brereton and Fred Rothwell (New York: Dover, 2005).

5. Samuel Beckett, *Complete Dramatic Works* (London: Faber, 1986).

6. Henri Bergson, *Creative Evolution,* trans. Arthur Mitchell (New York: Modern Library, 1911).

7. Losev, quoted in Hilary Fink, *Bergson and Russian Modernism, 1900–1930* (Evanston, IL: Northwestern University Press, 1999), 1; Richard Lehan, *The Crisis in Modernism: Bergson and the Vitalist Controversy* (Cambridge, UK: Cambridge University Press, 1992), 323; Samuel Alexander, *Space, Time, and Deity* (London: Macmillan, 1920), 220; Windham Lewis, *Time and Western Man* (London: Chatto, 1927), 166.

8. Anthony Uhlmann, "Image and Intuition in Beckett's *Film,*" *Substance* 33, no. 2 (2001): 90.

9. Charles Darwin, *The Autobiography of Charles Darwin, 1809–1882,* ed. Nora Barlow (New York: Collins, 1958), 139.

10. Fink, *Bergson and Russian Modernism,* 4, quoting from R. C. Grogin, *The Bergsonian Controversy in France, 1900–1914* (Calgary: University of Calgary, 1988); and Virginia Woolf, *The Common Reader* (New York: Harcourt, 1925), 212.

11. Irwin Edman, foreword to Henri Bergson, *Creative Evolution* (Westport, CT: Greenwood Press, 1975), xiv; Fink, *Bergson and Russian Modernism,* 4; and William James, quoted in Fink, *Bergson and Russian Modernism,* 1.

12. Bergson, *Creative Evolution,* 3, 4.

13. Ibid., 4.

14. Ibid., 5, 6.

15. James Knowlson, *Damned to Fame: The Life of Samuel Beckett* (London: Bloomsbury, 1996), 727n15.

16. Uhlmann, "Image and Intuition in Beckett's *Film,*" 94.

17. Unpublished paper by Christopher Morrison. The paper also suggests the following: (1) emphasizing their strange detachment, the universe around the tramps is subject to sudden fluctuations of "mechanical" time; (2) Pozzo and Lucky represent elements of mechanical time and *la durée,* respectively; (3) on many levels Beckett is toying with the idea of two consecutive, apparently iden-

tical, "moments" and how memory influences how the characters experience the second of these in light of their experience of the first.

18. Bergson's own examples tend to be of his era and not "politically correct." He wonders, for example, why "we" laugh at hunchbacks.

19. Bergson, *Laughter*, 18.

20. Vivian Mercier, *Beckett/Beckett* (Oxford: Oxford University Press, 1977), 163.

21. Quotes from *Film* taken from Beckett, *Complete Dramatic Works*, 323.

22. Bergson, *Laughter*, 28–29, 17. For the purposes of this essay, which concludes with an analysis of a wordless dramaticule, I ignore those parts of *Laughter* concerned with the linguistic games Cohn noticed in early Beckett.

23. Bergson, *Laughter*, 38. Bergson's description of the jack-in-the-box brings to mind Lucky's action during his monologue in *Waiting for Godot*: "Now, let us think of a spring that is rather of a moral type, an idea that is first expressed, then repressed, and then repressed again; a stream of words that bursts forth, is checked, and keeps on starting afresh" (35).

24. Bergson, *Laughter*, 39–41. Sully Prudhomme, quoted in *Laughter*, 39.

25. *Act without Words I*, in Beckett, *Complete Dramatic Works*, 206.

26. Ackerley and Gontarski, *The Grove Companion to Samuel Beckett*, 4.

27. Bergson, *Laughter*, 29.

28. Ibid., 4; "avoid any comic interpretation," from a conversation with Talish Barrow, Madison, WI, Dec. 2006; Bergson, *Laughter*, 6.

29. *Act without Words I*, 205.

30. Bergson, *Laughter*, 20.

31. George Politzer, "After the Death of M. Bergson," *La pensée libre*, no. 1, Feb. 1941, in *Ecrits 1: La philosophie et les mythes*, ed. Jacques Debouzy (Paris: Éditions Sociales, 1969). Mitch Abidor's English translation of Politzer's article is available at www.marxists.org/archive/politzer/works/1941/bergson.htm (accessed Nov. 28, 2007).

"The Ptydepe Word Meaning 'Wombat' Has 319 Letters"

An Information-Age View of Technology and Satire in the Works of Václav Havel

E. Bert Wallace

MOTORMORPHOSIS, a sketch written during 1960 and 1961 by a young Václav Havel, was written as one part of a three-act evening of absurdist cabaret called *Autostop* (or *Hitchhiking*). In Havel's contribution a group called "The Enemies of Motorism" gathers to hear a lecture by the renowned Professor Macek, director of the Motormorphological Institute of the Second Faculty of the Polyclinic. The meeting's Facilitator,[1] obviously having little sense of what's going on, opens the evening by insisting on creating an "informal atmosphere" while the professor feebly attempts to begin his lecture. Eventually, after a scolding from the Facilitator for procrastinating, the professor enlightens us about his field:

> PROFESSOR. Motormorphosis is, essentially, the phenomenon of pathological processes caused by psychoneurological problems which result in the slow and general transformation of a human into a car. . . . First the human skin self-polyurethanes. This is followed by the pneumatization of the human feet into tires, followed by the brakation of the human hands, followed by the carboratorization of the lungs, and the pistonization of the stomach. The motor muscles stiffen, bones transform into the chassis—at the same time, the function of the brain gradually disintegrates, up to the moment [of] motormortality.
> FACILITATOR. Isn't he sweet![2]

The sketch, though heavily rewritten and restructured by Ivan Vyskocil, was produced in Prague in 1961 at the Theatre on the Balustrade *(Divadlo na Zabradli)*, a force in the *mala divadla* ("small theatre") movement. It has been suggested that without the *mala divadla,* the Czech Revolution of 1990 could not have happened.[3] I will not join the considerable throng examining the overtly political importance of Havel's work.[4] Nor will I linger too long on Havel's existential treatment of Soviet-style bureaucracy (as in *The Garden Party*) or attempt to illuminate his (regrettably) nontheatrical writings of the last twenty years. I do suggest that, from his earliest through his most recent plays, Havel shows an interest in the comic possibilities of unchecked fascination with and unwarranted faith in technology as a means to human perfection and social progress. Specifically, machines of varying descriptions in *Motormorphosis, The Increased Difficulty of Concentration, The Memorandum,* and *Redevelopment* are employed to contemplate the "crisis of modernity" at the heart of Havel's plays.[5] Furthermore, this recurring theme will be shown as a factor in the relevance of these cold war plays to young, modern audiences.

The 2006 Havel Festival in New York produced "for the first time anywhere the complete plays of Václav Havel," including the world premiere of *Motormorphosis,* newly translated by Carol Rocamora and never before produced as originally written.[6] In *Motormorphosis* Havel deals explicitly with consumerism and technological fascination, leading ultimately to dehumanizing transformations clearly influenced by early exposure to Kafka and Ionesco.[7] Though those gathered to hear the lecture are "Enemies of Motorism," they can't help but be fascinated by the machines they ostensibly loathe. One speaks of his hatred of all things automotive, all the while using the language of cars: "I'm moving full-speed ahead to the future . . . er, walking full-speed ahead, that is." Another says he hates cars, but "only the driving part." He's a mechanic who can think of nothing but disassembling and repairing the machines. Yet another has an ill-defined feminist objection to cars: "I'm here to keep an eye on the men." As Professor Macek describes all the various eponymous syndromes relating to the disease ("Macek Vibration," "Macek automotorhypnosis," and so forth), the audience quickly moves from a theoretical objection to cars to an actual enthrallment with the motormorphic process. As in *Rhinoceros,* they all ultimately transform into the objects that initially disgusted them. The production consisted entirely of Czech-style marionettes, the transformations rendered at once surreal and quite literal.[8]

The sketch is just that—a sketch, not a fully realized play. Rocamora reports that Vyskocil recognized this and didn't hesitate to rewrite it (as a one-man show starring himself) for the original loose, cabaret-style production.[9] Furthermore, says Rocamora, "Havel did not take these collaborative works seriously and does not consider them a significant part of his oeuvre" (ibid., 36). Still, this early play demonstrates a clear link to the Theatre of the Absurd. Rocamora notes this early connection: "For Havel—and this is crucial to understanding his work—it was not so much that the theater of the absurd was an influence or a literary tradition or a 'tendency' (his term) that he sought to emulate. Rather, as he put it, absurdity was 'something that was in the air.' He meant this in a dual sense, referring both to the influences of Western writings that were passed around the table at the Café Slavia in the late 1950s, and to the reality of life in Czechoslovakia" (ibid., 393).

Of course, the similarity of *Motormorphosis* to *The Metamorphosis* and *Rhinoceros* is clear. Yet, while those plays exhibit animals as the organic "other" into which characters are transformed, Havel chooses the metal and rubber and polyurethane of the automobile. Is it funnier to see— or imagine—a woman turning into a car than it is to see a man become a cockroach? That's debatable. What is clear, however, is that Havel exploits the rather basic comic potential of his automotive situation while at the same time commenting on the absurdity of modern life "in the air" all around us.

The Increased Difficulty of Concentration, written in 1968 during the Prague Spring, focuses on technology in a different and perhaps more modernist way. The play fragments a day in the life of Dr. Eduard Huml— one of the many rather vague "social scientists" that people Havel's plays. Though more scholarly attention has been paid to Dr. Huml's sexual activities and attitudes, equally interesting among the chaos of this particular day in Huml's life is the unexpected arrival of yet another social scientist, Dr. Ana Balcar, and her team of technicians. They have chosen Huml at random for analysis as part of a very ambitious project. The two colleagues discuss the research:

HUML. I'd be interested to know the exact procedure you use in shaping human personality.
BALCAR. Well, we proceed from the following logical proposition: if men are related by the general aspects of their personalities, they must necessarily, on the other hand, be differentiated by those aspects which are particular and random. In other words, the gravitational focus of human individuality does not lie in any aspects which can be established as predictable, but, on the contrary, in those which defy all laws, all norms, and thus constitutes precisely the vast and neglected sphere of coincidence.
HUML. It sounds convincing. But how can one cope with this sphere— scientifically, I mean?[10]

Enter Puzuk. Puzuk has already been described by Balcar as "a small automatic calculator, model CA-213, suitably adapted to our needs, of course" (ibid., 34). Since the play is presented nonchronologically, the audience has already seen Puzuk in action (though exactly what was be-

ing attempted is initially unclear). The stage directions in Vera Blackwell's translation describe Puzuk as "a complicated piece of machinery,
faintly reminiscent of a cash register and/or a calculator. It is furnished
with a keyboard, various pushbuttons, a small crank on one side, and
eyepiece not unlike that of a microscope, a red and green bulb, a small
loudspeaker, and a long cord with a plug" (7).

Despite a crew of four, Puzuk never works properly. He's too hot, he's
too cold, he's too tired to gather the necessary data. He complains endlessly, both with loud warning sirens and in an "effeminate voice" (26).
At the end of the day, after being warmed, cooled, reasoned with, mas-
saged, and otherwise coddled, Puzuk goes berserk, repeatedly asking absurd questions ranging from "Where did you bury the dog" to "Do you
piss in public, or just now and then?" (50).

Czech scholar Jan Culik notes that "paradoxically, the 'Puzuk' com-
puter is the only 'human' individuality amongst the dehumanised and
mechanised 'scholars.'"[11] Indeed. Huml, though apparently respected,
is completely ineffectual. He repeats the same empty phrases to both
wife and mistress. He dictates a chapter ("Regarding Values") that is a
mixture of esoteric, academic jargon and platitudes that he completely
ignores in his own life. Dr. Balcar's team is a poorly meshed, four-gear
mechanism, including a Technician who dully records every conceivable
measure in Havel's apartment (including the weight of the bedclothes),
an Operator who argues peevishly with Puzuk, a Supervisor who does
nothing and constantly threatens to stop doing it, and Balcar herself,
who at first appears thoroughly professional but ends the play by weeping in Huml's arms and becoming his next mistress. Puzuk alone presents the possibility of efficiency and stability, a high-tech solution to
age-old questions. But again, he never actually works. The hope placed
in technology is baseless and absurd.

Perhaps better known, *The Memorandum* focuses on another modern
mechanism: the efficiently functioning office. Ptydepe, a "synthetic language, built on a strictly scientific basis," has been constructed to create "maximum efficiency" in the workplace. But its rules are hopelessly
complex as taught by Lear, the corporate trainer: "The significant aim of
Ptydepe is to guarantee to every statement, by purposefully limiting all
similarities between individual words, a degree of precision, reliability,
and equivocation quite unattainable in any natural language. To achieve
this, Ptydepe makes use of the following postulation: if similarities between any two words are to be minimized, the words must be formed
by the least probable combination of letters. . . . The greater the redundancy of a language, the more reliable it is. . . . How does, in fact,
Ptydepe achieve its high redundancy? By consistent use of the so-called
60 percent dissimilarity." And so on. Appropriately enough, Lear's les-

son begins with the ominous line, "There are many months of intensive study ahead of you." Gross, our hero, spends the play trying fruitlessly to have a memo translated using this modern innovation. Eventually, Ptydepe is deemed unworkable, the very things that were heralded as its strengths declared its weaknesses.[12]

Havel is well known for his satires of bureaucracies. But Ptydepe takes bureaucracy to new heights (or depths, as the case may be). It is the product of modern thought, of a positivism that optimistically believes that humanity is perfectible—here through the use of technology as applied to language. Praised as far superior to any "natural" language, Ptydepe is as clunky and unworkable as Puzuk (whom one can imagine as the inventor of the language). But hope springs eternal in the hearts of middle management as Chorudor, a new and improved interoffice language, is enthusiastically introduced at the end of the play. As Gross laments, "Manipulated, automatized, made into a fetish, Man loses the experience of his own totality; horrified, he stares as a stranger at himself, unable not to be what he is not, nor to be what he is" (ibid., 129).

Redevelopment, Havel's penultimate play (to date), was written in 1987, just as the cracks in the Iron Curtain were beginning to show. The technological salvation presented by the "Institute" here is modern architecture and urban planning. The architects are certain their plans to modernize the "old castle town" will usher it into the modern age; the citizens of the town are uninterested in being so ushered. A series of Inspectors arrive and make contradictory proclamations. The leaders of the protest movement are imprisoned (shades of Havel's own experience). Near the end of the play, the most vocal leader is broken, and another commits suicide. The play ends with a moving speech by Bergman, the redevelopment project director: "We are all responsible for the sad shape our world is in, which has hounded a sensitive man beyond the limits of his endurance. We're callous, indolent, indifferent, deaf to the voices of those near and dear to us and blind to their pain. . . . Let us vow never again to connive in the 'redevelopment' of the souls of ourselves and others."[13]

Redevelopment is "an overtly political metaphor about perestroika," written at least in part as a reaction to a visit to Czechoslovakia by Mikhail Gorbachev.[14] It has atypical elements for Havel, such as the lone, Chorus-like violinist playing pointedly Russian music and the only suicide in any Havel play.[15] But even in this later work Havel focuses on the absurdity of hope in technology—in this case, architecture and modern notions of the proper physical environment as key to human advancement.

But what does all this use of technology mean to the modern audience? Particularly, why are younger audiences in the United States, for whom the fall of the Berlin Wall and the Velvet Revolution are dim childhood memories, interested in a cold war Czech poet-king? Havel's plays are regularly staged at American universities—though this could be explained by the interests of faculty directors rather than students. Still, Havel's recent residency at Columbia generated significant student interest. Student actors and audience members engaged enthusiastically in my recent production of *The Increased Difficulty of Concentration* with little if any knowledge of Havel as a playwright or historical figure. Though no attempt is made here to deemphasize other qualities of Havel's plays, it is his use of technology that specifically resonates with the Information Generation because of its unique relationship to technology.

Cell phones, iPods, and the Internet, which today's students take as an unquestioned and necessary part of the human experience, in fact dehumanize while promising utopia. Each of these examples of the most modern technology ostensibly furthers the human race by connecting us all in a benevolent Web. But the isolation that is highlighted by Puzuk and Ptydepe parallels the growing phenomenon of students walking across campus talking not to one another but to some removed "other" or merely drifting along in their own personally designed musical miasma. Users of modern "information and communication technologies" ("ICTs," a nice Havelian acronym) have been described as having an "absent presence," a concept easily applied to Havel's disconnected, existentially adrift characters. Though he probably isn't listening to himself, Dr. Huml makes the following observation as he dictates a chapter:

> There exist situations—for example in some advanced western countries—in which all the basic human needs have been satisfied and still people are not happy—they experience feelings of depression, boredom, frustration, and so forth—full stop. In these situations, man begins to desire that which in fact he perhaps does not need at all—he simply persuades himself he has certain needs which he does not have—or he vaguely desires something which he cannot specify and thus cannot strive for—full stop. Hence, as soon as man has satisfied one need—i.e., achieved happiness—another so far unsatisfied need is born in him, so that every happiness is always simultaneously a negation of happiness.[16]

The nature of the technology produced by the modern equivalent of "advanced western countries" renders it almost instantly obsolete. Perceived needs—for faster processors, for bigger flash drives, for smaller and smaller devices to do everything—are met and immediately felt again. Because young audiences can relate to Havel's characters, they are drawn to his plays.

It's not difficult to imagine a new Havel tragicomedy—perhaps titled

Cellular Fusion—in which characters once again transform into grotesque figures. With hands welded to ears and eyes glued to tiny screens, they dance incongruously to inaudible music while frantically typing with their elbows on impossibly small keypads. Endlessly buying and throwing away gadget after gadget, they repeatedly shout, "You're breaking up!" to no one in particular.

Notes

1. The title is literally translated "Inaugurator." Translator Carol Rocamora notes that "Facilitator," with all its connotations, is a more dynamically equivalent American translation. See note 2, below.

2. Václav Havel, *Motormorphosis,* trans. Carol Rocamora and Tomas Rychetsky, unpublished translation, 2006.

3. See Olga F. Chtiguel, "Without Theatre, the Czechoslovak Revolution Could Not Have Been Won," *TDR* 34, no. 3 (fall 1990): 88–96.

4. For more on this subject see D. Christopher Brooks, "The Art of the Political: Havel's Dramatic Literature as Political Theory," *East European Quarterly* 34, no. 4 (Jan. 2006): 491–522.

5. On the "crisis of modernity" see James F. Pontuso, *Václav Havel: Civic Responsibility in the Postmodern Age* (New York: Rowman and Littlefield, 2004), 71.

6. "Celebrating the Life and Art of Václav Havel," Untitled Theater Company #61, www.untitledtheater.com/havel/havel-festival.html (accessed Nov. 25, 2007).

7. Carol Rocamora, *Acts of Courage: Václav Havel's Life in the Theater* (Hanover, NH: Smith and Kraus, 2004), 34.

8. All quotations from Havel, *Motormorphosis.*

9. Rocamora, *Acts of Courage,* 33.

10. Václav Havel, *The Increased Difficulty of Concentration,* trans. Vera Blackwell (New York: Samuel French, 1976), 46.

11. Jan Culik, "Václav Havel," www.arts.gla.ac.uk/Slavonic/havel.html (accessed Nov. 25, 2007).

12. All quotations from Václav Havel, *The Garden Party and Other Plays* (New York: Grove Press, 1993), 65–67.

13. Quoted in Rocamora, *Acts of Courage,* 265.

14. Ibid., 266.

15. Ibid., 265.

16. Havel, *The Increased Difficulty of Concentration,* 30.

Terry Johnson's *Hysteria*

Laughter on the Abyss of Insight

Luc Gilleman

Nothing is funnier than unhappiness, I grant you that.
—Nell in Samuel Beckett's *Endgame*

Semiotic Plenitude

"If you are waiting for me to break the silence you will be deeply disappointed. The silence is yours alone, and is far more eloquent than you imagine."[1] These are the opening lines of *Hysteria or Fragments of an Analysis of an Obsessional Neurosis,* Terry Johnson's hilarious account of the meeting that took place between Sigmund Freud and Salvador Dalí in London, in July 1938, shortly before Kristallnacht and a little more than a year before the outbreak of World War II. The audience has been looking at an old man dozing in a chair. When he suddenly speaks, his words never fail to startle, until the audience realizes it is not being addressed. Laughter relieves the tension. The audience has just been introduced to the power game and inconsistencies of psychoanalysis—the patronizing attitude of the therapist and the contradictions involved in the therapeutic transaction, as Freud is the one breaking the silence while denying he is doing so.

Freud realizes he is alone in his study and moves to his desk to alert his daughter Anna, a psychoanalyst herself and here an offstage figure supposedly at the other end of the intercom. It is the middle of the night, and he is confused about a newly installed light pull that dangles in front of him, "a four-foot cord with a brass knob on the end":

FREUD. [. . . .] What's this thing?
....
ANNA. What thing?
FREUD. This thing in my hand.

ANNA. Um . . .
FREUD. It's just dangling here. It's got a knob on the end.
ANNA. Mmm hmm?
FREUD. What am I supposed to do with it?
ANNA. Shall I call the nurse?
FREUD. Shall I give it a pull?
ANNA. No, just . . . leave it alone, father.
He pulls it. The lights go out.
FREUD. Scheisse! (2)

In theatre, where ideas and situations have to unfold quickly, opening scenes are crucial. Here, too, information is closely packed as, beat by beat, hints are dropped about what is to come. Nothing is random—not even the choice of the expletive "Scheisse" (shit), which Freud repeats several times in the play. It is an ironic reminder that he is no stranger to the "anal obsessions" he ascribes to the English after watching a performance of Ben Travers's *Rookery Nook*. If "English farce," as he concludes, has a "seductive logic" (9), so has psychoanalysis. *Hysteria* makes good use of this similarity, linking the saturation of meaning that is typical of farce, a particularly tightly edited genre, to the semiotic plenitude that is one of the basic assumptions of psychoanalysis and, later, through the figure of Dalí, to the hyperconscious representations typical of surrealistic art.

As Freud tugs at the light pull, darkness briefly descends, and laughter marks another site of unarticulated meaning. The audience has already experienced the power game and contradictions of psychoanalysis. That it is obsessed with sex only confirms a common prejudice. But the scene also suggests something less obvious yet central to the play's argument, concerning the relationship between illumination and the phallus: when Freud sheds light on the darker regions of his patients' minds, he does so as a man—not objectively, but with a primary allegiance to his gender.

Freud, then, is not a larger-than-life figure, Dante's vision of a Virgil who leads us through our own personal underworld. In the play he stands revealed as a fallible man, limited in his masculine point of view and therefore prone to fail, to hurt as much as to heal—and with this perception of human vulnerability the gloom of tragedy descends on a play that starts in laughter and ends in tears. After this scene Freud lies down on his famous couch, a visual reminder of the origin of psychoanalysis in solipsistic monologue, in Freud talking and listening to himself in the yearlong and later censored self-analysis that followed his father's death in 1896. The dream he tells is his famous account of the anxiety that accompanies waiting for a train: "I prepare and prepare and yet remain unprepared, because when the train arrives there will be no time to button the jacket or check the ticket or even say a meaningful goodbye. So until my inevitably fraught departure all I can [do] is wait, and re-arrange the luggage" (3). The audience's attention has been shifted from sex to death and the pressing issue of unfinished business. At that point a young woman appears at Freud's window. She is a particularly troublesome piece in Freud's luggage that, while he is waiting for the inevitable train, will require vigorous rearranging. Standing in the rain, in the dark, she comes with a complaint and insists on a hearing—setting off the intrigue that propels the action in what is still Johnson's most successful play.

"Charnel-House Joker"

Terry Johnson is the odd man out in British theatre. Born in 1956, he gained recognition in the 1980s when a few of his plays were being produced at the Royal Court and the Bush Theatre. These were the Thatcher years—for British theatre a time of issue-based, mainly social realistic, state-of-the-nation plays—many of them written by women: Michelene Wandor, Liz Lochhead, Pam Gems, Sarah Daniels, and Timberlake Wertenbaker, for instance. This was not a good time for laughs, yet that is when Johnson started to make a name for himself with an improbable comedy called *Insignificance,* about Marilyn Monroe explaining relativity theory to Einstein and Joe McCarthy confiscating Einstein's only copy of the Unified Field Theory. It was successful enough to be turned into a movie by Nicolas Roeg a few years later. Still, no one seemed to know what to make of Johnson. At a time when so many playwrights wrote with evangelical zeal, the best thing that could be said about him was also the worst thing that can be said of any artist—namely, that he was a master craftsman, an engineer of theatrical space and time, a good clockmaker.

A decade later, critical opinions of Terry Johnson had shifted. The 1990s in Britain saw the emergence of a new generation of angry young playwrights, many of them male, who wrote "In-Yer-Face Theatre," grim, often violent, and despairing plays. But it was also a time of the rediscovery of the theatrical space, of its endless possibilities, and of spectacular design. The production that marked the decade was, rather improbably, J. B. Priestley's 1946 play *An Inspector Calls,* dusted off and newly varnished by Stephen Daldry in 1992. A year later the competition for that play was Johnson's *Hysteria,* first staged at the Royal Court Theatre on August 26, 1993, and then transferred to the Duke of York's on November 24, 1995. Like *An Inspector Calls,* it requires spectacular stage design and has enjoyed numerous productions worldwide.[2] As in *Insig-*

nificance, it features a chance meeting between greats, this time Sigmund Freud and Salvador Dalí. In the 1990s, a decade of doom and gloom, Johnson was suddenly no longer a clockmaker but a grinning moralist—or, as Nicholas Wright puts it, a "twentieth-century Jacobean; original, tragic, a charnel-house joker." Johnson, says Wright, is a Puritan, fascinated by sex and death, the dual destinies of the flesh.[3]

Mixing dramatic genres has become Johnson's hallmark, signaled, for instance, in the title of the aptly named *Dead Funny* (1994), where a fan club of frustrated men and one desperately accommodating woman gathers to remember the passing of the misogynist British comedy idol Benny Hill. Plays in which the serious and the funny are less judiciously mixed, such as *Cries from the Mammal House* (1984) and *Imagine Drowning* (1992), reveal Johnson's sentimentality—at times, even mawkishness. In *Cries from the Mammal House* he laments the loss of a common humanity and preaches against the dangers of solipsism: "My compassion and my pity and my caring is all for me. No one else," says Alan in an awkwardly melodramatic scene that ends with his suicide.[4] And through Buddy in *Imagine Drowning* (1991) Johnson advocates the healing effects of compassion: "Ocean's all around you, boy, whether you like it or not. Only compassion will keep you afloat!"[5] This comes all too close to the "easy sentimentality" Peter Brook warned against in *The Empty Space.* Johnson admitted in an interview that it was "undeniably the worst thing I've ever written."[6] This longing for a shared humanity and a wholeness of being is present in all of his plays, but in the best of them, including *Hysteria,* Johnson establishes a conflict between what is said and what is shown, often inviting laughter where tears would be more appropriate. This perversity of intent is what makes his plays interesting, though also frustrating and perhaps even a little mean. In *Unsuitable for Adults* (1984), a play that features a feminist stand-up comedian, one character opines that "being funny isn't about being funny at all; it's really about being really, really, nasty."[7] One suspects as much from Johnson.

As few other plays, *Hysteria* raises the question of the relationship between farce and tragedy, laughter and insight. Freud is dying from cancer of the jaw, and we are laughing at a dying man's visions, expressive of his disquiet and fear. As Wright reminds us, "Laughter in adults is generally a function of terror, shame or *Schadenfreude:* it seldom has much to do with happiness. And laughter in Johnson's plays is ironic, even a touch grotesque: it's like a pair of inverted commas within which a highly Jacobean masque of mortality is acted out."[8] Laughter grows uneasy when in the final act the set becomes Daliesque: Freud, tortured by his conscience, wants to escape, but the clock melts, the phone turns into a lobster, and the door handle becomes elastic. And laughter ceases when the grotesque images that well up from Freud's unconscious—representations of his doubt, guilt, and fear—assume the shape of four naked women, the sisters Freud left behind in Vienna when he fled to London and who, after his death, will perish in extermination camps. In the course of a few hours the play moves from comedy and farce to surrealistic horror and tragedy.

Hide and Seek

In *Hysteria* much of the audience's laughter is the product of farce, of a deft handling of theatrical space and time. In farce, says Terry Hodgson, characters are "like jugglers. The situation grows ever more complicated and the actors juggle faster to keep the play, like a ball, in the air. The audience watches, holds its breath and laughs when a ball almost drops."[9] Freud's juggling abilities are put to the test in *Hysteria*. Abraham Yahuda, his London physician, is determined to prevent the publication of his atheistic tract *Moses and Monotheism* (1939); the unpredictable Salvador Dalí has chosen this day to pay him a visit; and there's a naked young woman hiding in his closet. What a Jewish doctor, a crazy Spanish artist, and a naked woman have in common, and why Freud tries to prevent two of them from meeting, we figure out in the course of the play. In the meantime the result is laughter, as Freud shunts these three in and out of rooms and concocts ever more improbable interpretations to make an unpredictable reality comply with his vision of it. At one particularly desperate moment the old Freud is even compelled to execute a vigorous Cossack dance in an unlikely game of charades.

Juggling is as good a metaphor as any for what farce is all about. But there are others, more attuned to a play that features a woman taking her clothes off. The Swedish playwright Lars Norén once suggested that in drama something is covered up only so that it can be gradually revealed.[10] In other words drama is a little like striptease. In farce that game of covering and uncovering, hiding and exposing—the very mechanism of playwriting—becomes the subject of the play. In this case the mechanism is also thematically relevant. "I have nothing to hide," says Johnson's Freud. "Indeed, to hide nothing has been my sole quest" (58). The historical Freud is supposed to have been the master of exposure, who stripped the bourgeoisie of its pretenses, convinced it that there was no safe hiding place for its secrets. As he says in *Dora: A Case of Hysteria,* "He that has eyes to see and ears to hear may convince himself that no mortal can keep a secret. If his lips are silent, he chatters with his fingertips; betrayal oozes out of him at every pore. And thus the task of mak-

to climax and recognition *(anagnorisis)* is thus made to echo the covering and uncovering that in psychoanalysis is known as the "return of the repressed." The talking cure is supposed to bring relief or, as Freud puts it, to turn the miserable into the merely unhappy. But, as Jessica says to Freud, "Because I can articulate these things does not mean I am able to bear them" (78). Neither, in fact, can Freud, who with an act of self-censure nails himself back on the cross of psychoanalysis. I am no longer a man, he says; I am a museum. I am not weeping; "the exhibits are screaming" (78).

The "comic," says Ionesco, "is an intuitive perception of the absurd, it seems to me more hopeless than the 'tragic.'"[19] *Hysteria* confirms this grim view. Only near the end of the play do we realize that *Hysteria* is not a morality tale pitching the good woman against the evil man but that Jessica is the voice of Freud's conscience. The play offers a vision of knowledge as a farcical oscillation between covering and uncovering, hiding and exposing—or a continuous shunting and rearranging that will only end with death. In Johnson's grim view the never-ending process of covering, uncovering, and recovering—a return of repression following the return of the repressed—assumes absurdist overtones. It is a Sisyphean, zero-sum operation that Freud is doomed to repeat until he dies. At the end of the play, heavily sedated by morphine, he is sitting alone in his chair, awaiting the knock on the window and another battle with the woman in his closet.

Notes

1. Terry Johnson, *Hysteria or Fragments of an Analysis of an Obsessional Neurosis,* rev. ed. (London: Methuen, 1995), 1. Subsequent references will be cited parenthetically by page number in the text.

2. The play was originally directed by Phyllida Lloyd, who also directed its American premiere at the Mark Taper forum for the 1994–95 season. In 1999–2000 another famous production was directed by John Malkovich for Chicago's Steppenwolf Theatre. Two years later the play premiered in a French version by Lulu and Mike Sadler, also directed by Malkovich, at the Marigny Theater, in Paris, before moving to Barcelona.

3. Nicholas Wright, "Is man no more than this?" introduction to *Plays: 2,* by Terry Johnson (London: Methuen, 1998), xi, viii.

4. Terry Johnson, *Cries from the Mammal House,* in *Plays: 1* (London: Methuen, 1993), 198.

5. Terry Johnson, *Imagine Drowning,* in *Plays: 2* (London: Methuen, 1998), 77.

6. See Peter Brook, *The Empty Space* (New York: Atheneum, 1983), 72–73; Terry Johnson, interview by Charles Spencer, *Daily Telegraph,* June 7, 1995, quoted in Margaret Llewellyn-Jones, "Terry Johnson," *Dictionary of Literary Bi-*

ography, vol. 233, *British and Irish Dramatists since World War II,* 2nd ser., ed. John Bull (Detroit, MI: Gale Group, 2001), 177.

7. Terry Johnson, *Unsuitable for Adults,* in *Plays: One* (London: Methuen, 1993), 70.

8. Wright, "Is man no more than this?" ix.

9. Terry Hodgson, *The Drama Dictionary* (New York: New Amsterdam Books, 1988), 130.

10. Lars Norén, "'Es passiert mehr in meinem Leben, wenn ich schreibe . . .': Auszüge aus Gesprächen mit Lars Norén," *Nacht, Mutter des Tages,* by Lars Norén, trans. Angelika Gundlach, Programmbuch no. 84 (Wien: Burgtheater, 1991), 26.

11. Sigmund Freud, *Dora: An Analysis of a Case of Hysteria,* ed. Philip Rieff (New York: Macmillan, 1963), 96.

12. Sigmund Freud, *Wit and Its Relation to the Unconscious,* in *The Basic Writings of Sigmund Freud,* trans. A. A. Brill (New York: Random House, 1938), 634, 771. James Strachey translates the original title *Der Witz und seine Beziehung zum Unbewussten* (1905) as *Jokes and Their Relation to the Unconscious.*

13. Christophe Campos, "Traduire le théâtre: Hystérie à quatre mains," *Franco-British Studies: Journal of the British Institute in Paris* 32 (2003): 66.

14. Bernadette Rey-Flaud, *La farce ou la machine à rire: Théorie d'un genre dramatique, 1450–1550* (Genève: Librairie Droz, 1984), 297.

15. Freud, *Wit and Its Relation to the Unconscious,* 776.

16. Ibid., 778.

17. Hodgson, *The Drama Dictionary,* 35.

18. In this respect the play is very much like D. M. Thomas's *Eating Pavlova* (1994), a fictional account that also centers on the seduction theory and contains explicit references to Masson's accusations. Incidentally, in some productions Yahuda gives the sleeping Freud a shot of morphine at the beginning of the play. This way the audience is given a hint that the events Freud experiences may be hallucinations, which may make the play a little less troubling.

19. Eugène Ionesco, *Notes and Counternotes,* trans. Donald Watson (London: John Calder, 1964), 25. Quoted and discussed in Verna A. Foster, *The Name and Nature of Tragicomedy* (Burlington, VT: Ashgate, 2004), 32.

Situations, Happenings, Gatherings, Laughter

Emergent British Stand-Up Comedy in Sociopolitical Context

Broderick D. V. Chow

The "Weather Vane"

As we analyze stand-up comedy, it is important we remember that it is a "popular" form, perhaps from some perspectives a "low" form. It is, by definition, entertaining. Stand-up comedy may be edifying, challenging, subversive, or educative, but it need not be any of these things. What it *needs* to be is funny. There is great value in a cultural form with such entertainment appeal yet that frequently contains all the above secondary characteristics. Cultural historians trace the direct roots of the modern form of stand-up comedy to commercial entertainment (vaudeville and music-hall),[1] yet even in the infancy of the form comedians were already using the potential of direct address to tackle social or political issues, to express rage or affection for their society, in short, to give reason to the laughter. This can be seen in the existence of the "chitlin circuit" alongside the mainstream in America, in which black comedians had license to say what was otherwise forbidden, or the resentful bigotry of many working men's club comics in 1970s Britain. British audiences, in particular, have seen the rise of alternative comedy, a highly politicized incarnation of the form. Far from being "mere entertainment," stand-up comedians are fully aware of the power of their art form and strive to do justice to what Tony Allen (the oft-labeled "Grandfather of Alternative Comedy") cites as their anthropological forebears: the Fool, the Jester, the Shaman.[2] Because the form places the performer as both writer and medium in a central position, stand-up comedy acts as a social and political weather vane; the comedian's art is located in the reception by an audience of what Christopher Ritchie describes as a comic's "Micro-World," a unique and personal point of view of the world expressed through a series of jokes.[3]

In this essay I detail a specific cultural shift in British stand-up comedy: the popularization of late 1970s to 1980s alternative comedy, a politically charged form of comedy emerging in the early days of Margaret Thatcher's administration, the diffusion of its radical aspects, and the emergence of a new form with a different but no less important political utility—the growth of performer-centric, comedian-generated clubs that embody a do-it-yourself ethic. For ease of use, I will refer to this newer genre as "Do-It-Yourself" (or DIY) comedy for its aesthetic, as well as its relationship to other movements aimed at reclaiming or creating one's own cultural experience. My theoretical framework for discussing this emergent form's political function is "relational art" and Nicholas Bourriard's theory of relational aesthetics.[4] I begin with a definition of DIY comedy as an alternative to the mainstream, in contrast to "alternative comedy" as a period-specific genre of stand-up. I then detail the theory of relational aesthetics and situate the functional aspects of stand-up within that theory. My purpose is to show that the proliferation of DIY events in comedy is analogous to the wider range of relational/situational events created in response to a social sphere ailing through the dominance of global capitalism and that DIY comedy represents an exemplary form of response to these events.

Two caveats must be considered. The first is location. My research is focused entirely on London's comedy circuit, which, due to its size and pluralist nature, allows enough like-minded individuals to come together to form legitimate "scenes." The project provides, however, a methodology of analysis applicable to other cultural milieus, such as similar emergent scenes in New York or Los Angeles. The second caveat is my own position within the project. I began as a surveyor, outlining a cultural process and a theoretical framework. Because, however, I am a comedian performing on London's circuit, my own practice and insights thereof must be brought to bear. The first part of the essay investigates *what* is happening and the second *how* it is happening.

The Residual and the Emergent

The audience members gathered in the bar of the Battersea Arts Centre in South London quickly finish their drinks and file into the small studio space. They are greeted, individually, by an excited, friendly young woman of twenty-four, the comedian they've come to see, who urges them to take a photocopied, hand-drawn magazine she has made and directs them to a table on which there are homemade cardboard badges and a makeshift polling box. The badges are a gift for the audience. Beside the polling box are small slips of paper. The comedian asks the audience to write on these their "Favourite Small Thing" and drop the slip into the box. The house lights dim (though not so much as to create palpable distance between audience and performer), and the comedian introduces herself and the show. She then shares what, over hundreds of performances, her favorite audience "Favourite Small Thing" has been: "I like to pretend gang members are holding hands." This is, essentially, the beginning of Josie Long's show *Kindness and Exuberance*. The specifics change nightly, but this program of interaction and participation remains constant. The effect is surprisingly touching, calling to mind the image of Long taking the box home and revealing the treasures inside. In an interview I later conducted, Long explained the impetus behind this opening engagement with the audience: "You do get people coming into the gig, quite cynical, maybe even by accident, but you get people to do these things and they sort of light up—they get really childish again."[5] Josie Long, winner of the 2006 *if.commeddie* award for Best Newcomer, is one of the central figures in the postalternative alternative.

Raymond Williams's triptych of analytical paradigms—the Dominant, Residual, and Emergent[6]—is helpful in looking at the cultural shift from an agitprop-influenced, anti-Thatcher 1980s alternative, to a comedy-saturated Britain in the 1990s, to a diversified entertainment market post-2000 and an emergent DIY ethos. Nearly thirty years have passed since the alternative comedy movement was born. The term is generally attributed to Tony Allen, who denies having coined it, despite having pulled together a group of comedians and cabaret performers under the name Alternative Cabaret.[7] I should make it clear that many of the ad hoc, performer-motivated characteristics of DIY comedy are virtually identical to those of alternative comedy (at least, initially); Oliver Double writes, "It's not misty-eyed romanticism to say that the first generation of alternative comedians weren't in it for the money. The fact was that there was very little money involved at all."[8] The cultural shift of stand-up comedy in Great Britain points to a continuous drive to reclaim comedy as a performer-driven art form, challenged by its own nature as an entertainment "product." Both alternative comedy and emergent DIY comedy oppose a dominant culture of mainstream comedy that reduces or constrains comedians according to how their work may be consumed or disseminated.

Alternative comedy is today largely a meaningless term, like *alternative music* or *indie rock*, having lost its meaning through widespread popularity. Roger Wilmut and Peter Rosengard note in their survey of the history of alternative comedy that even in 1979, in the early days of the genre, the label was already contentious: "'Alternative Comedy' is a phrase that few of those involved in that area of comedy in Britain seem to like."[9] What was alternative comedy an alternative *to*, then? In some respects the style was an alternative to the easy but offensive racist or sexist material proffered by mainstream television or club comics of the time (Bernard Manning's hate-filled one-liners, for example, are often cited as anathema to alternative comedy).[10] It was also an alternative to the apolitical, nonsensical style that emerged from Victorian music hall and variety and had remained a hallmark of British comedy since: "a purely theatrical entertainment . . . with the comic emphasis on nonsense rather than social realism."[11] With the opening of the London Comedy Store coinciding with Margaret Thatcher's rise to power, alternative comedians had their satirical guns trained on the new conservative government: "Political satire was an important part of their style, but usually looking at the way the behaviour of the government directly affected the audience, especially in terms of the then rapidly rising unemployment and increasing poverty among young people in particular" (ibid., xiv). One can argue, however, that alternative comedy was merely an alternative to a culture that did not value or emphasize comedy as performed onstage, with the increasing ubiquity of television comedy. As Tony Allen remarks, it "filled a vacuum" left by a mainstream that was out of touch with a younger, postpunk generation.[12] Many of the rooms that allowed alternative comedy to exist (the Comedy Store, Jongleurs, Banana Cabaret) are now considered mainstream venues, clubs that give comedians their first break on a career path toward television and film success. During the last thirty years or so, alternative comedy, once the emergent, has become the mainstream, the concerns and impetus behind it now residually extant. Raymond Williams's essay "Base and Superstructure in Marxist Cultural Theory" provides a simple explanation of alternative comedy's gradual assimilation into (or, *of*) the mainstream: "In capitalist practice, if the thing is not making a profit, or if it is not being widely circulated, then it can for some time be overlooked, at least while it remains alternative. When it becomes oppositional in an explicit way, it does, of course, get approached or attacked."[13] Peter Rosengard, founder of the Comedy Store, was known for his entrepreneurship; in

1999 the club, now run by Don Ward, who was involved since its inception, was turning a profit of more than £2.5 million[14]—so perhaps the alternative that was given free reign to play by Rosengard's venue was always fated to become the mainstream.

The cultural dominance of the alternative comedy genre today in no way means that its initial impetus and concerns have followed suit. Steve Bennett, who runs the online comedy reviewing Web site *Chortle* discusses the terminological confusion that follows words such as *alternative* and *mainstream:* "In one club, a young black comic positions himself in front of the dark backdrop and asks: 'Can you see me?' . . . 120 miles away, a comic pledges support for striking firefighters, and calls for higher taxes for the rich. . . . But the audience that was so delighted with that standard 'black' line was at The Comedy Store, the venue synonymous with the birth of politically-correct alternative comedy. And the second comic was Bernard Manning."[15] Josie Long makes a similar claim:

> I think it's really diversified. I think it's sort of, basically, maybe twenty years ago . . . you had people defining themselves against the "comedians," like, proper "mother-in-law, dress shirt . . ." that sort of people, so you did have two clear divisions. But now it's much more complicated. It's like second- and third-wave feminism. You've got backlashes and stuff like that. What I consider to be the established alternative comedy venues . . . I really consider those mainstream. So there's a lot of people who consider themselves alternative comedians who just aren't.[16]

This confusion of alternative and mainstream is not only problematic because it makes labeling difficult. The mainstream is dominated today by "British Comedy" as a saleable product, reflected in the expected career path of any new comedian; hundreds of unpaid "open spots" (unless this is bypassed through success in one of many competitions), to "paid 20s" (paid twenty-minute performances) in smaller venues, to supporting or compering established rooms, headlining, touring, and, eventually, television and film success. Clubs such as the Jongleurs and, to a lesser degree, the Comedy Store deliberately market to office parties or hen nights (bachelorette parties) and utilize the "laughs-per-minute" ratio to determine how well the comedian has performed. There is little room for experimentation, let alone error; comedy is a product to be sold alongside chicken in a basket and alcohol. Considered in light of Tony Allen's description of alternative-comedy vanguard Alexei Sayle's performances at the early Comedy Store ("His only material was a handful

of short, exquisitely written first person anecdotes about artistic or political arguments he'd had in unlikely settings"),[17] my earlier statement
about the meaninglessness of the alternative label seems justified.

Enter the emergent. The instability of the name *alternative* makes me
wary of employing it in description of a new style. Instead, I employ
"Do-It-Yourself comedy," which reflects the return to the performer-
driven creative impetus of early alternative. Defiantly grassroots in intentionality, it can be defined as the sum of a number of (mostly London-
based) comedy clubs that are generated by performers. Mainly these
take place in rooms above pubs or bars (though this is hardly prescriptive but borne out of economic necessity; Laughter in Odd Places uses
found spaces as its venues). Loosely grouped together in a scene, DIY
clubs and performers inhabit a nexus of shared intentionality. There is a
"misfit" quality to most of these clubs and a drive to create one's own
cultural experience. Many clubs are run at a loss or break even and experiment outside of the "three acts + a compere" structure of mainstream clubs. Although there is no singular style, DIY comics tend to
be less confrontational and more inclusive than others, engaging with
the audience outside of the standard heckle/put-down ritual. The most
prominent of these clubs in London is Robin Ince's Book Club. Ince
created this club in order to perform comedy that was literary and particular to audiences as book-loving as he. The Book Club is often described as a cult favorite, with a small but loyal following—a scene. It
generally loads the bill with an enormous number of acts (sometimes
upward of twelve), features readings from pulp and romance novels,
and offers physical comedy experiments including accordion accompa-
niment and musical numbers. Josie Long's the Sunday Night Adventure
Club even more explicitly engages with the DIY ethic. It is a themed
evening, with handmade decorations and souvenirs to match (themes
have included in the past "Pirates v. Ninjas—Who's the Best?," crafts,
and the Mighty Ducks). Long engages with the audience outside the
standard rituals of stand-up comedy. Audiences in front rows of comedy
rooms often fear being made fun of by the compere; Long tries to "calm
people down. . . . 'I'm not going to pick on you, and insult you.'"[18] Instead, the engagement with the audience comes from games (including
live Boggle competitions) and simple nonthreatening and unadorned
conversation. Other clubs include the OK Club with Les Marsh, the
Comedian's Graveyard (a monthly club whose theme is, cleverly, death
and dying), Notsvig's (once Toksvig's until its founder, Caroline Clif-
ford, received a phone call from Sandi Toksvig's agent), and Laughter in
Odd Places (which has performed comedy in launderettes, libraries, Ox-
fam shops, and Hampstead Heath). The DIY club, unlike other comedy

clubs, is not a means to another end, such as a national tour or television showcase. It is in itself a goal, created to engage audiences with a sense of fun and unpredictability. Unlike alternative comedy, which opposed a singular mainstream with a mostly defined style, the mainstream of 2007 is stylistically diverse and primarily defined in commercial terms— it is whatever operates within the structures that sell. Put simply, the form of DIY comedy is anathema to large comedy rooms, which thrive on quick succession of acts with numerous breaks for the purchase of food and drink. While "The Store" will always remain the birthplace of alternative comedy, today there is little room for comedians who do not fit its "laughs-per-minute" ratio or require the audience to actively engage with them.

I have defined both alternative and DIY comedy as emergent, using Williams's term: "By 'emergent' I mean, first, that new meanings and values, new practices, new significances and experiences, are continually being created."[19] We can establish with some certainty that both practices have emerged out of dissatisfaction with the constraints of the mainstream at the time, but the values of these mainstreams, and thus the values of the two genres themselves, are quite different. Alternative comedy emerged, at least in part, from social boundaries and controls, whereas DIY comedy has emerged from an increasing sense of purpose-lessness and loneliness among young persons in Western society.

Wilmut and Rosengard note that the early performers populating the Comedy Store in 1979 "came not from the small comedy circuit then struggling into life, but from the more established world of fringe theatre,"[20] such as Tony Allen's performance group Rough Theatre, which in itself emerged from a landmark loosening of authority: the abolition of theatrical censorship by the Lord Chamberlain's office. Thus, subversive political satire, smut, "blue" (read: foul) language, and other afore-thought unsavory characteristics poured into fringe theatre, as well as the burgeoning alternative. The relaxing of socially imposed restraints also contributed to the alternative comedy ethos. Tony Allen, in response to an exercise with Rough Theatre in which each actor was given half a day to discuss themselves and their sexuality, says, "It seemed a whole generation of men and women with hapless uptight parents had fumbled their way through adolescence and blundered in and out of relationships and failed to deal with any of it, until they'd got some distance and a few good experiences behind them."[21] It is not difficult to see the openly sexual comedy of Jo Brand or Jenny Éclair as spring-boarding from this generational confusion.

This generation finds itself in a very different position. Most DIY comics are between the ages of nineteen and thirty-five, having witnessed conflict, 9/11, and the destructive power of globalization through the lens of media, television, video games, and the Internet. Cynicism, irony, and a knowing awareness to formal experimentation are calling cards of its art and entertainment, as is the feeling of being lost or alone. During the Southeastern Theatre Conference in Morgantown, West Virginia, this year, I discussed this generational distinction with a twenty-something improviser and MA student from Austin, Texas, named Erica Lies, who described today's laughter response as "apocalyptic": "It's the sense that everything that happens to us is so apocalyptic that the only thing we *can* do is laugh at it." There is a trend toward irony, or, more accurately, exposing as absurd our own response to tragedy, in DIY comedy. In her six-minute set at Robin Ince's Book Club at Battersea Arts Centre in February 2007, Jo Neary took on Anne Frank and teenage angst in the same line, quoting from her own diary at age ten: "My diary will be just like Anne Frank's, though, hopefully, more exciting!" This joke is arguably insensitive, yet its target is its author, not Anne Frank, though Neary assumes a knowing, ironic response on the part of the audience. A number of emerging comics also deal with the theme of loneliness and alienation; Terry Saunders's show *Pulp Boy* told the story of a misfit teenager who decides to speak entirely in lyrics by Jarvis Cocker's band Pulp, while his show for the 2007 Edinburgh Festival is called *Missed Connections* and deals with the titular form of advertisements placed in newspaper classified pages. Daniel Kitson is considered in many ways an innovator with his storytelling shows, which Josie Long describes:

> Dan Kitson does these shows that are about love and loneliness, and they're so heartfelt, and if you connect with him, what you're really doing is you're saying, "I've felt that." . . . And so, as a result, by watching it, and by connecting with it you are put in a position of being quite vulnerable—like you've been moved into this place you're a bit uncertain to be a part of.[22]

Ben Thompson, who in his book *Sunshine on Putty* contentiously outlines a Golden Age of Comedy with Vic Reeves on one side and *The Office* on the other, unfairly argues that post–"Golden Age" comedy "lack(s) a crucial element of moral focus."[23] Several times the student-protest roots of the alternative comedians are cited. While DIY comedy may not express a prescriptive morality in its content, it expresses an important humanist morality of inclusion and human agency. DIY comedy attempts to create unique cultural experiences through human interaction.

Relational Aesthetics: A Different Approach to Art and Performance

Relational aesthetics is a critical theory put forth by Nicholas Bourriard and views the sole function of art as the enabling of relationships with the world and among humans. Relational aesthetics dismisses critical frameworks based on the narrative of "art history," in which value is based on the reiteration of signs, forms, or objects from the past. Rather than evaluating artwork on the reappearance and exchange of a particular sign or trope, we are urged to focus on the moment or action of sign exchange itself. Relational art is the exemplary medium to apply this approach, defined by Bourriard as "[a] set of artistic practices which take as their theoretical and practical point of departure the whole of human relations and their social context, rather than an independent and private space."[24]

A good example is Alix Lambert's *Wedding Project,* in which the artist was married and subsequently divorced six times. This series of relationships was represented by a gallery display featuring the detritus of the marriages. But in such relational art it is difficult to locate *where* the "finished" art object is. The gallery items are souvenirs—relational aesthetics would rather consider the artwork as an accretion of exchanges, in the ideological forum Lambert has created through her actions within an existing social system. Relational art is at once ephemeral and composed of concrete, "actual" human behaviors. It draws attention to the fact that any complete art object (sculpture, painting, ready-made) is a representational object for the artist's modus operandi, exchanging signs (which are then interpreted) with the viewer—a "Trace" (Bourriard's term) as opposed to relational art's "Programme."

DIY comedy is the execution of the comic form that exemplifies the role of relational art: "no longer to form imaginary and utopian realities, but to actually be ways of living and models of action within the existing real."[25] It breaks away from comedy as consumable and passive leisure product and remakes it into an active, participatory event. DIY comedy emphasizes the event as a whole; the goal is to execute the Programme. It is more akin to a party than a show and in this way is aligned with nontheatrical "happenings" aimed at reclaiming socializing and public space—FlashMobs, such as Mobile Clubbing or Pillow Fight, and O'Donnell's *Social Acupuncture* experiments in Toronto.[26]

Why are these important? Bourriard points to the idea of the Society of Extras, derived from Guy Debord's *The Society of Spectacle,* in which all persons are urged to participate minimally in the spectacle; reality television, viral videos, and blogging are all aspects of this paradigm. This participation enables citizens to feel some semblance of agency without actual participation in effective structures of society: "The ideal subject of the society of extras is thus reduced to the condition of a consumer of time and space. . . . Before long, it will not be possible to maintain relationships between people outside (these) trading areas."[27] Bourriard, like so many others, is frustrated by the presentation of consumer choice as the only form of choice.

In the context of *The Society of Extras,* in which social intercourse is minimal and virtual, the creation of performance with the goal of enabling such social relationships has great political utility. Thus a comedian is potentially an activist par excellence, using a blanket of techniques I call "relational work." Stand-up comedy, lacking a fourth wall, is a unique scenario of social interaction in which the quotidian face-to-face encounter is enlarged in scale and placed under the aegis of "entertainment." Thus, the comedian faces the scenario of "holding forth at the dining table," magnified exponentially. The hallmark of a great comedian has long been his or her ability to improvise, and in the absence of the fourth-wall, improvisation begins to look a lot like everyday conversation.

Oliver Double teaches practical stand-up comedy to fourth-year drama students at the University of Kent. One exercise, known as Microphone Conversations, simply involves one participant standing behind a standard microphone and conversing with the audience. The audience asks questions; the comedian may or may not answer these and is welcome to pose questions to the audience as well. While stand-up is often viewed as a magical, mysterious process, Double's exercises, which I have participated in on a number of occasions, demystify stand-up; in essence, it becomes the simplifying of one's presentation of self to humorous elements (as defined by reception with one's audience). "Presentation of self" here alludes to the work of sociologist Erving Goffman, who argues that performance in everyday life utilizes "sign-vehicles" or "sign-equipment" in order to define the encounter at hand and control its outcome.[28] The encounter between the stand-up comedian and audience member is an active use of sign-vehicles that form a comedian's *persona* (as well as audience "signing"—laughter, heckles, deliberate silence) in order to define the terms of the situation and its outcome. Both parties attempt to establish a social contract that allows laughter to exist. In my own stand-up, superficial sign-vehicles include my physical appearance and dress sense, my accent, gesturing with my hands, and body language. Less conscious sign-vehicles relate to the comic's Micro-World;[29] in this case my microworld is defined by my habit of presenting intel-

ligent topics of conversation and subverting them in a strikingly ignorant way. Double's microphone conversation exercise begins casual and
conversational, and the workshop leader emphasizes that the comedian
is under no pressure to be funny. As the comic begins to "score-points,"
shoring up laughter, the comic's flow of dialogue hones in on "just the
funny bits." The comic builds his or her relationship with the audience
through relational work, establishing a social contract in which his or her
jokes may be received as pleasing and funny.

The instability of the encounter is central to stand-up comedy (after
all, part of the danger and lure of stand-up is the foreknowledge that
perhaps no one will laugh). The encounter itself is unique in its expectation of direct performer-audience intercourse. By relocating the place of
encounter from everyday spaces (afternoon coffee, watercooler, dinner
table) to the comedy club or black-box theatre, stand-up comedy denies
its participants the stable rituals or signs that define an encounter in familiar space. DIY comedy's political potential is the release of social exchange from spaces of consumption with no other specific aim (in other
words, without the secondary intention of career pursuits or "to be on
television") than to create an event or situation in which other people
participate under the banner of fun and pleasure.

By invoking the ghost of Raymond Williams earlier, I ran the risk of
falling into one of two traps. Either I am subconsciously fetishizing the
grassroots alternative of DIY comedy—as part of what Michael Bérubé
calls a "Marxist Culture Chart . . . according to which cultural practices are weighed in the scales and valued chiefly (or exclusively) for
their degrees of cool radical emergentness and even cooler resistance to
incorporation"[30]—or I am guilty of placing far too much importance
on a drop in an ocean and should resist labeling anything as emergent
before it has shown considerable oppositional or resisting power to the
dominant.[31]

Despite these concerns, however, I believe DIY comedy is a legitimate
response to a current cultural climate in which there is almost limitless
choice in leisure or entertainment products yet a growing dissatisfaction
with them. Like other movements aimed at reclaiming cultural capital
both past (punk music, fanzines) and present, DIY comedy is available
for incorporation into the mainstream—yet being a form whose existence relies so heavily on networks or scenes of like-minded individuals,
small audiences, and a desire to form relationships through performance,
it is difficult to conceive of a mainstream version of DIY comedy. Stephen
Duncombe defends the study of DIY subcultures (in this case, zines):
"While zines themselves may be relatively unimportant, the implications
of this DIY ideal are huge. What would happen if we all decided to pro-

duce politics in this way?"[32] If the goal of much activism is to empower civil society, then surely the desire to create one's own entertainment or cultural experience is an act of subversion.

Richard Schechner's famous "entertainment/efficacy braid" is one of the more common models invoked by those studying or involved with "political performance." But as our culture becomes increasingly viral, made up of lateral, rather than vertical, cultural influence, what is efficacious performance? Any attempts to "ritualize performance, to make theatre yield efficacious acts,"[33] are generally viewed as suspect—or (perhaps justifiably) pretentious. To return to the notion that opened this essay—that is, of stand-up as entertainment—I wish to argue that stand-up comedy need not define itself as simply entertaining or strive to be efficacious. It is an efficacious act because it is so entertaining. In the context of a society in which simple social intercourse is so difficult, stand-up comedy as practiced in DIY clubs—let's forget for a moment Jongleurs, *Have I Got News For You,* and Comedy Central—performs the "actual" of face-to-face communication, something that is becoming increasingly "virtual." A comedian goes out and talks to strangers every night, something many find difficult or intimidating. As Darren O'Donnell notes, however, talking to strangers is crucial to creating and maintaining a "healthy, functioning social sphere."[34] Regarding his relational art project the Talking Creature, an experiment in talking with strangers, O'Donnell writes: "We were about to do something that, according to the great myth of liberal democracy, should be a comfortable given, but in reality it's horribly nerve-wracking, throwing into question the very idea that we live in a democracy. If this place is so democratic, why can't strangers talk freely?"[35]

Notes

1. This refers mainly to British stand-up comedy; American stand-up comedy has had an earlier, if slightly different, path of development. See Oliver Double, *Stand-Up! On Being a Comedian* (London: Methuen, 1997); and Tony Allen, *Attitude—Wanna Make Something of It? The Secret of Stand-Up Comedy* (Glastonbury, UK: Gothic Image, 2002).

2. See Allen, *Attitude—Wanna Make Something of It?*

3. Christopher Ritchie, "Stand-Up Comedy and Everyday Life" (PhD diss., University of London, 1998).

4. Nicholas Bourriard, *Relational Aesthetics,* trans. Simon Pleasance and Fronza Woods with Mathieu Copeland (Dijon-Quetigny: Les Presses du Reel, 2002).

5. Josie Long, interview by the author, April 29, 2007.

6. See Raymond Williams, *Culture and Materialism: Selected Essays* (London: Verso, 1980), esp. 31–49.

7. Allen, *Attitude—Wanna Make Something of It?*

8. Double, *Stand-Up!* 221.

9. Roger Wilmut and Peter Rosengard, *Didn't You Kill My Mother-in-Law? The Story of Alternative Comedy in Britain from the Comedy Store to Saturday Live* (London: Methuen, 1989), xiii.

10. See Steve Bennett, "Bernard Manning," *Chortle* (2002), www.chortle.co.uk/comics/b/3136/bernard_manning (accessed May 11, 2007).

11. Wilmut and Rosengard, *Didn't You Kill My Mother-in-Law?* xiii.

12. Allen, *Attitude—Wanna Make Something of It?* 39.

13. Williams, *Culture and Materialism*, 43.

14. Oliver Double, *Getting the Joke: The Inner Workings of Stand-Up Comedy* (London: Methuen, 2005), 82.

15. Bennett, "Bernard Manning."

16. Long, interview.

17. Allen, *Attitude—Wanna Make Something of It?* 97.

18. Long, interview.

19. Williams, *Culture and Materialism*, 41.

20. Wilmut and Rosengard, *Didn't You Kill My Mother-in-Law?* 20.

21. Allen, *Attitude—Wanna Make Something of It?* 89.

22. Long, interview.

23. Ben Thompson, *Sunshine on Putty: The Golden Age of British Comedy from Vic Reeves to "The Office"* (London: Fourth Estate, 2004), 435.

24. Bourriard, *Relational Aesthetics*, 113.

25. Ibid., 13.

26. Darren O'Donnell, *Social Acupuncture: A Guide to Suicide, Performance, and Utopia* (Toronto: Coach House Books, 2004).

27. Bourriard, *Relational Aesthetics*, 9.

28. See Erving Goffman, *The Presentation of Self in Everyday Life* (London: Mayflower, 1959), esp. 1–18.

29. Ritchie, "Stand-Up Comedy and Everyday Life."

30. Michael Bérubé, "Theory Tuesday, Act V Scene iii," www.michaelberube.com/index.php/weblog/theory_tuesday_act_v_scene_iii/ (accessed April 10, 2007).

31. See Williams, *Culture and Materialism*.

32. Quoted in Amy Spencer, *DIY: The Rise of Lo-Fi Culture* (London: Marion Boyars, 2005), 37.

33. Richard Schechner, *Performance Theory*, 2nd ed. (London: Routledge, 2003), 121.

34. O'Donnell, *Social Acupuncture*, 49.

35. Ibid., 53.

Contributors

Steven Dedalus Burch received his graduate degrees from Northern Illinois University and his doctorate from the University of Wisconsin-Madison and is the theatre historian at the University of Alabama. He has written and published on theatre of the Holocaust and on the plays of Harold Pinter and Lee Blessing. His book, *Historical Invisibility: Andrew P. Wilson and Irish and Scottish Theatres, 1911–1950*, is to be published in early 2008 by the Edwin Mellen Press.

Patrick Bynane has worked professionally as a teacher, actor, director, and technician in North Carolina, Louisiana, Missouri, and Ohio. Dr. Bynane is an assistant professor of drama at Texas Woman's University in Denton, where he advises the department's MA candidates and teaches theatre history, literature, and dramatic structure, as well as the introductory theatre course. He received his PhD in Theatre History/Criticism from Louisiana State University in 2002.

Diana Calderazzo is a PhD candidate and Teaching Fellow in Theatre Arts at the University of Pittsburgh, focusing on cognitive studies and drama therapy. She received her MA degree from the University of Central Florida and her BA degree from Smith College. Much of Diana's recent research focuses on the musicals of Stephen Sondheim, and her article on cognitive audience reception of the 2005 Broadway revival of *Sweeney Todd* can be found in the fall 2007 issue of the *Sondheim Review*.

Broderick D. V. Chow is currently completing the first year of his PhD at Central School of Speech and Drama, University of London, the first specialist college of drama and performing arts under the University of London banner and home to the Centre for Excellence in Theatre Training. His research looks at stand-up comedy as a "relational" form of performance, focused on the network of social relationships that exist between the spotlight and the seats. Broderick is a stand-up comedian, actor, and comedy writer. He can be seen on the London comedy circuit, as well as further afield in the United Kingdom. He has just finished a run of *Akira California,* a practical inquiry through stand-up and storytelling at the Camden Fringe, and CSSD's Festival of Emergent Art. He also runs the monthly comedy club Justice League of Comedy, which is a themed night devoted to comic books and superheroes.

Luc Gilleman teaches modern drama and literature courses in the English department and the Comparative Literature program at Smith College. His publications include articles on British and American playwrights, and he is the author of *John Osborne: Vituperative Artist* (New York: Routledge, 2002).

Stanley Vincent Longman is Professor Emeritus, Department of Theatre and Film Studies, University of Georgia. His major research interests are dramatic analysis and criticism and Italian theatre. He is the author of *Composing Drama* (1986) and *Page and Stage* (2004), both published by Allyn & Bacon. He has also published articles on Italian theatre history with particular emphasis on the evolution of Italianate theatre architecture from the Renaissance into the eighteenth century. He has translated plays by such playwrights as Carlo Goldoni, Carlo Gozzi, Pietro Chirari, Luigi Pirandello, Luigi Antonelli, Rosso di San Secondo, Dino Buzzati, Luigi Lunari, and Luisella Sala.

Christopher Morrison moved to Wisconsin in 2006 to work on a PhD in Theatre at the University of Wisconsin-Madison. Having grown up in Northern Ireland, his connection to the professional stage began as organist in Sondheim's *A Little Night Music* at Belfast's Lyric Theatre. He has completed master's degrees in journalism (Columbia University) and music composition (Cambridge University) and has taught in Japan, Saudi Arabia, Kuwait, England, France, and the United States. He hopes to write a dissertation on the influence of Bergson on Beckett.

Felicia J. Ruff is chair of the Department of Theatre and Speech at Wagner College in Staten Island, NY, where she teaches theatre history, script analysis, and seminars on Oscar Wilde and Greek theatre.

She spent the summer of 2007 at UCLA's NEH seminar, "The Oscar Wilde Archive."

Boris Senker is professor of drama and theatre in the Department of Comparative Literature at Zagreb University in Croatia, and editor-in-chief at the Lexicographical Institute in Zagreb. His publications include books on director's theatre, Croatian and European theatre of the twentieth century, Shakespeare on Croatian stages, theatre exchanges, and two volumes of theatre bibliography. He is the coauthor of twenty-five plays.

Biliana Stoytcheva-Horissian, MFA, PhD, serves as a department chair at Emory & Henry College, where she teaches acting and movement. An accomplished actor who has performed and conducted master classes nationally and internationally, she has presented papers and numerous acting workshops at regional and national conferences. She has recently published an article on audition monologues in the *Players' Journal* and conducted a workshop on comic acting at the ATHE national conference in New Orleans. Her research and artistic interests include comedy, Molière, acting pedagogy, and Eastern European absurdism. Some of her acting credits include *Magic Voices, Blood Wedding, The School for Wives, Period of Adjustment,* and *A Midsummer Night's Dream.* Recently she has appeared in *Collected Stories,* produced by Paradox Ensemble Theatre.

E. Bert Wallace is an assistant professor of theatre at Campbell University in Buies Creek, North Carolina, where he teaches theatre history, directing, and playwriting. He is also a director and dramaturg, as well as codirector of the University Honors Program.